Home Office

HM PRISON SERVICE

Special Units for Long-Term Prisoners: Regimes, Management and Research

A Report by the Research and Advisory Group on the Long-Term Prison System

LONDON: HER MAJESTY'S STATIONERY OFFICE

FOREWORD BY THE HOME SECRETARY

When the Report of the Control Review Committee was published in July 1984 it was widely welcomed as an important and imaginative contribution to public debate about the problems posed by long-term imprisonment. Its recommendations have been energetically pursued by my Department. One of the developments to which we have attached particular weight was the establishment of the Research and Advisory Group on the Long-Term Prison System to provide the Prison Department with advice on the research needs arising from the CRC Report and, in particular, to advise on the proposed special units for long-term prisoners.

The Research and Advisory Group has now produced a progress report setting out its advice to the Prison Department on the special unit strategy and the associated research needs. As the CRC recommended, the Group includes outside academics among its members. This form of partnership with the academic community has been a stimulating new departure for the Prison Department and I would like to take this opportunity to express my thanks to the outside participants who have made such a valuable contribution to the thoughts contained in this Report.

Among the most difficult and challenging issues any prison service has to face is the question of how it responds to the control problems posed by some long-term prisoners. In publishing this Report we do not seek to present the Research and Advisory Group's thoughts as the final word on the subject. Rather, we hope that the Report will encourage further informed discussion of a hitherto somewhat neglected area. It is in this spirit that I commend the Report to readers both within and outside the Prison Service.

Rt Hon Douglas Hurd, CBE, MP

Contents

Introduction

In July 1984 the Home Office published a Report by the Control Review Committee (CRC) entitled *Managing the Long-Term Prison System*[1]. This Report recommended, as part of a package of recommendations, that a system of small units should be 'established to cater for prisoners who are identified as presenting control problems which cannot be dealt with in normal long-term prison conditions'.

2.   Following the publication of the CRC Report our Group — the Research and Advisory Group on the Long-Term Prison System (RAG) — was established by the then Home Secretary with the following terms of reference:

> 'To provide the Prison Department, on request, with a source of advice on the research needs arising from the report of the Control Review Committee, and how they may be met, and, in particular, to advise on the planning, co-ordination and evaluation of the proposed long-term prisoner units.'

Our membership is set out at Annex A.

3.   We met for the first time in November 1984. Since then we have concerned ourselves mainly with the development of a strategy for the establishment of the special units and with the identification of research needs. This report is a progress report setting out our advice to the Prison Department on both these matters.

---

1.   HMSO, July 1984 (*CRC Report*)

1
Background

The Control Review Committee (CRC)

4. In September 1983 the then Home Secretary established a working party, the Control Review Committee, with the following terms of reference:

> 'To review the maintenance of control in the prison system, including the implications for physical security, with particular reference to the dispersal system, and to make recommendations.'

5. The Control Review Committee's members were a mixture of Prison Department officials and senior prison governors. In their Report — *Managing the Long-Term Prison System* — the Committee reviewed the long history of serious disturbances and riots which the dispersal prisons had experienced. The Report noted that, in general, the existing dispersal prisons do not lend themselves to dealing with prisoners in small groups; that they tend to operate an undifferentiated regime for prisoners on ordinary location; and that the combination of the open regime[2] and relatively large units that characterise dispersal prisons make these establishments particularly vulnerable to disruption. It also identified a lack of sufficient incentives to long-term prisoners to behave well and of disincentives to bad behaviour, and a lack of facilities for dealing with long-term prisoners who persistently present disruptive behaviour in dispersal prisons.

6. The CRC concluded:

> 'There will inevitably be control problems if long-term prisoners are held in a system that gives inconsistent messages about the course of their sentences or the consequences of their actions, and if prison managers' only recourse in the face of disruption is to switch prisoners between normal location and the segregation unit, and between one prison and another.'

(CRC Report, paragraph 133)

The CRC's Recommendations

'New generation' designs and the future of the dispersal system

7. In the light of their analysis the CRC concluded that:

---

2. The CRC used the term 'open regime' to describe the quality of life that a long-term high security prison system should, in their view, try to offer. They defined such a regime as 'one that offers a range of constructive activities, the opportunity of association, and supervision by staff who have the time and training to take a personal interest in each inmate as an individual'. The term 'open regime' is used in the same way throughout this report.

'We are sure that the May Committee[3] were right to be sceptical about the positive benefits of the dispersal concept. It is a very expensive business to run eight prisons at the highest possible level of security. And there are real operational problems in mixing Category A prisoners among a much larger number of inmates with lower security requirements. Although Category A prisoners are subject to special security procedures that do not apply to the rest of the population, it would be impossible to devise any workable arrangements that enabled that group to be treated as a self-contained problem. A prison population cannot be compartmentalised in that way in the existing plant. This means, to put it crudely, that the inherent tension in prisons between security and control is accentuated in dispersals.'

(CRC Report, paragraph 7)

They added that 'the dispersal system seems a precariously balanced structure to carry our hopes into the next century'[4]. They accordingly considered whether, in the long term, there was any practicable alternative to the policy of dispersal.

8. The Committee concluded that the arguments would inevitably end in favour of dispersal rather than concentration so long as the debate was conducted within the constraints dictated by existing concepts of prison design. They went on to say, however, that the 'new generation' of prison designs current in the USA appeared to bring a new dimension to the dispersal versus concentration debate:

'Prisons that are made up of self-contained units in the 'new generation' style obviously have an in-built capacity to separate groups of prisoners. They also offer great flexibility since the units need not all be run in the same way and may be operated in as separate or concerted a manner as the operational situation requires... We think that our requirement for very high security accommodation is unlikely to be more than 300–400 and it would appear that, if 'new generation' prison designs are indeed successful, this number could be held in two small prisons of the new generation kind without incurring the disadvantages that we have noted as being inherent in dispersal policy. We therefore recommend that these possibilities are urgently examined...

...We do not flatly recommend the replacement of the dispersal system by a small number of 'new generation' prisons, since that concept of prison design has still to be evaluated in the UK. Nevertheless, we do not conceal our hope that this is the way in which the matter will develop.'

(CRC Report, paragraphs 20 and 127)

9. The Committee recognised, however, that in the short to medium term such radical changes were clearly not available. They therefore recommended a strategy of two complementary sets of initiatives which they considered would improve and support the existing long-term prison system (and which they believed would remain valid even if the dispersal system were replaced by 'new generation' prisons).

Planning long-term prisoners' sentences

10. First, they proposed a package of recommendations designed to improve the structure of the long-term prison system in a way that would encourage the

---

3. See the *Report of the Committee of Inquiry into the United Kingdom Prison Services* (Cmnd. 7673, 1979).

4. CRC Report, paragraph 127.

prisoner to co-operate, rather than the reverse, and would send the prisoner the right signals about the connection between his behaviour and the course of his prison career. They considered that this could best be achieved by giving all long-term prisoners (whom they defined as those serving over five years) *individual career plans* which would be drawn up after a thorough assessment in sentence planning units in local prisons at the beginning of the prisoner's sentence. These career plans would relate the different stages of a prisoner's sentence to each other in a meaningful way; they would incorporate goals which the prisoner concerned perceived as desirable because they would be tailored to his particular needs and hopes; and the achievement of these goals would be explicitly related to the prisoner's behaviour. The Committee also considered that, in order to make the most of sentence planning, *central allocation* should be introduced for all long-term prisoners (again defined as those serving over five years).

11.   The Committee believed that the introduction of central allocation would greatly improve the 'ability to get long-term prisoners to the right part of the prison system at the right time of their sentence'. But they were also concerned that security categorisation was insufficiently objective and that this produced an inbuilt tendency to over-categorise and thus slow the progress of long-termers towards the lower security establishments. They therefore recommended in addition that the Department should move towards *a more objectively based security categorisation system*[5].

12.   The Committee went on to say that, although sentence planning and central allocation would go a long way towards ensuring that the system sent prisoners the right signals, they would not by themselves provide the complete solution:

'Central control of allocation to establishments whose roles are not centrally planned and defined would represent an improvement on the present state of affairs, but the proposition has only to be stated in that way for its limitations to be obvious...We believe that the intelligibility that we want to see in the prison system can be achieved only by, first, formulating national policy aims; second, setting objectives and priorities for individual establishments within the overall plan; and, third, developing the machinery to monitor the success with which objectives are attained.'

(CRC Report, paragraphs 89 and 90)

13.   In this context the CRC recommended that there should be 'a move towards *individual programmes* for prisoners, incorporating more diverse activity than at present and geared towards the abilities and needs of the inmate himself' and that '*incentives should be developed in Category C and D prisons* in order to make security down-grading and progression through the system a consistent and psychologically credible process'.

---

5.   See paragraphs 80–85 of the CRC Report.

The management of prisoners who persistently present serious control problems

14.   The Committee considered that the implementation of this package of recommendations as a whole would make the experience of long-term imprisonment more intelligible to prisoners and would help to prevent serious control problems arising with the majority of long-term prisoners. They also considered, however, that, notwithstanding these reforms, there would almost certainly continue to be some long-termers whose behaviour would not respond to the inbuilt incentives of a better structured system, and who would continue to present a serious threat to the stability of the long-term prisons. The second line of development that the Committee recommended was, therefore, designed to address this problem.

15.   The existing options available to prison governors for dealing with long-term prisoners who are persistently disruptive are transfer to another establishment; transfer to a prison hospital (in the case of the mentally disturbed); or segregation under Rule 43 of the Prison Rules (either in his own establishment or on temporary transfer to another establishment under the terms of Circular Instruction 10/74[6]). In the Committee's view these options were all inadequate as long-term solutions. The CRC therefore recommended that the options should be increased by the establishment of a *system of small specialised units* designed to hold prisoners who persistently present serious control problems in the long-term prisons.

16.   The CRC did not attempt to specify exactly how many special units would be required nor precisely what their regimes or size should be. What they did say was that the units should offer a variety of regimes, and that at least one unit should be established (on the lines of the unit which had existed from 1970–1979 in C Wing at Parkhurst Prison) to provide a specialist facility for disruptive prisoners with some form of mental abnormality.

17.   In describing their conception of the units and the way in which they would operate the CRC said:

'...it must be clearly understood that the [special] units are not punitive in purpose. The primary aim will be the safe and humane containment of those who are unsuited to normal prison life, and, although very controlled conditions may sometimes be required to achieve that end, every effort should be made to ensure that the regime is as positive and supportive as possible...What is required...is some kind of facility midway between segregation and the ordinary wing, where prisoners who have difficulty with normal prison conditions can be helped to find ways of coping in

---

6.   Circular Instruction 10/74 provides that a dispersal prisoner may be removed from association under Rule 43 and transferred to a local prison for a period of up to 28 days with the intention that after that period (or before if the situation permits) he will return to his parent prison. This facility is available for a prisoner who 'needs to be removed from normal location because of an imminent explosive situation caused by either his actual or impending disruptive behaviour, and for whom placement in the segregation unit is inappropriate or impracticable, either because the prisoner would still be able to exercise a disruptive influence from the segregation unit (because of inadequate insulation between the segregation unit and the main prison) or because the extent to which the prisoner provides a focal point for prisoner unrest would mean that the mere act of placement in the segregation unit could have a provocative and explosive effect on the rest of the establishment'.

smaller, more supportive situations and then guided back into the mainstream when they are ready; and where the exceptionally dangerous prisoners in long-term segregation can gradually be tested out to discover what degree of freedom and association they can safely accept.'

(CRC Report, paragraphs 66 and 68)

They added:

'We strongly recommend that this should be done as a positive, developmental initiative, with outside academics participating in the planning and evaluation, and with as much openness as possible about the whole project.'

(CRC Report, paragraph 135)

The size of the dispersal system

18.   The CRC thought that the development of the special units would enable the dispersal sytem to be reduced in size. They suggested that the need for nine dispersal prisons had hitherto been argued partly on the basis that an adequate number of facilities was needed to separate undesirable groups of prisoners, and partly on the proposition that no one dispersal prison should have more than a small percentage of Category A prisoners. While agreeing that the ability to separate was important, the CRC did not accept the logic of any fixed proportion of Category A prisoners in any one establishment. They argued instead that it was the proportion of high *control* risk prisoners rather than of high *security* prisoners that was at issue, and that many inmates who required high security did not present a control threat while in prison. They considered that the establishment of special units would increase the capacity of the system to separate and control prisoners and would gradually reduce the proportion of control risk prisoners within the dispersal prisons; and they went on to say:

'We believe that the dispersal system should be reduced in size in response to the better situation on both separation and control that we are confident will be encouraged by the supporting facilities that we recommend. Taking account, too, of the increasing accommodation that is coming into full use at Frankland, we think that, as part of our scheme, two prisons should leave the dispersal systems. Wormwood Scrubs D Hall should clearly be one of these.'

(CRC Report, paragraph 129)

The importance of staff/prisoner relations

19.   The CRC also made what seem to us to be some very important general observations about the maintenance of control in prisons. They said:

'But our package of specific proposals is only part of the story. At the end of the day, nothing else that we can say will be as important as the general proposition that relations between staff and prisoners are at the heart of the whole prison system and that control and security flow from getting that relationship right. Prisons cannot be run by coercion: they depend on staff having a firm, confident and humane approach that enables them to maintain close contact with inmates without abrasive confrontation. Nothing can be allowed to qualify the need for staff to be in control at all times, but we are sure that the very great majority will agree with us that this is best achieved by the unobtrusive use of their professional skill at involvement with prisoners. This is the foundation on which we want to build.

6

We have not tried to analyse matters like the grievance procedures and the discipline system (which is, in any event, under review by a departmental committee). It is clear, however, that they have an important bearing on prisoners' perceptions of the fairness with which they are treated, and we are naturally aware that unanswered grievances and a sense of unfairness have often been found at the root of disorders in many countries and at many periods. All that we would say is that it is most important that both staff and inmates feel that they are getting a fair deal, and that all who live and work in a prison should have a stake in preserving its orderly management. We are not suggesting that there should be collusion with prisoners for the sake of a quiet life, but that it should be recognised that prisons function on humane personal relations between staff and inmates, and that there should be sensible reasons for rules and routines.'

(CRC Report, paragraphs 16 and 17)

Research

20. Finally, in addition to their specific recommendations, the CRC identified a general lack of research into prison control issues and recommended that a programme should be established with the help of outside academics to meet this need.

The Implementation of the CRC Report

21. When the CRC Report was published in July 1984 the then Home Secretary welcomed it as 'a positive agenda for establishing a better framework of control in our long-term prison system' (a view that was subsequently endorsed by the present Home Secretary). The Report had avoided simplistic solutions and offered a wide-ranging and complex package of recommendations, some elements of which will necessarily take several years to implement. A brief factual account of the progress that the Prison Department has made so far in implementing the CRC Report is given in paragraphs 22–28 below. (A full summary of the CRC's recommendations and their implementation to date is given in Annex B.)

The Research and Advisory Group on the Long-Term Prison System

22. One of the then Home Secretary's first actions after publication of the CRC Report was to establish our Group. As we said in paragraph 3 above, since our creation we have concerned ourselves mainly with the development of the special units and with research needs. It is intended, however, that we should begin to extend our work into other CRC-related areas in the year ahead.

Special units

23. The Prison Department has attached priority to establishing the special units in order to provide relief for the long-term prisons. The first unit opened at C Wing, Parkhurst on 30 December 1985 and now provides a facility for long-term prisoners who have a history of both troublesome prison behaviour *and* psychiatric illness or abnormality. A second special unit is scheduled to

open at Lincoln Prison in the first half of 1987 catering for prisoners who do not require psychiatric oversight. A third is planned to open at Hull Prison in early 1988, and the Department plans to establish further units in subsequent years. The development of the special units strategy has been taken forward with the assistance of this Group and is discussed in detail in Sections 2 and 4 of this Report.

Research

24. With our assistance the Prison Department has drawn up a research programme covering prison control issues. Our advice on this subject is set out in Section 3 of this Report and an account of the Prison Department research programme is given in Annex D.

Planning long-term prisoners' sentences

25. Since the CRC reported, the prison population has risen sharply and the local prisons in particular are now more hard-pressed than ever. In these circumstances the Prison Department has concluded that it is not practicable to require the local prisons to take on the additional burden of holding and assessing all long-term prisoners for 12 months after sentencing as the CRC proposed. The Department is currently re-assessing the merits, practicality and resource implications of the CRC's recommendations on sentence planning and central allocation of long-term prisoners. The Department is also reviewing security categorisation procedures with a view to moving towards a more objective categorisation system.

26. The Department acknowledges the force of the CRC's arguments for providing long-term prisoners with incentives to good behaviour and for developing incentives in Category C and D prisons in particular in order to make security down-grading and progression through the prison system a consistent and psychologically credible process. The present Home Secretary decided to begin with the provision of additional privileges in open prisons that will make it easier for prisoners to strengthen and retain their contacts with family and friends: since April 1986 there has been no limit on the number of letters prisoners in open establishments may send and receive; there are earlier and more frequent opportunities for home leave; and payphones to which prisoners have access are being installed. The Department accepts the logic of extending these privileges to Category C prisons, but it intends to evaluate the experience of these changes at open establishments before proceeding any further. This evaluation will take place in the context of a wider consideration of Category C and D regimes by a Prison Department working group which will begin early in 1987.

The size of the dispersal system

27. In February 1986 Hull Prison was taken out of the dispersal system and converted to a local prison. (About 25 dispersal prisoners, including Category As, will remain in A Wing at Hull until mid-1987.) When the new dispersal

8

prison, Full Sutton, opens in 1987 there will therefore be a total of eight dispersal prisons. The number of dispersal prisons will be kept under review by the Department as the special units develop, with particular reference to the CRC's recommedation that D Hall at Wormwood Scrubs should cease to have a dispersal role.

'New generation' designs and the future of the dispersal system

28.   Following the publication of the CRC Report, the then Home Secretary set up a working party and commissioned a detailed study of the US 'new generation' prison designs and their relevance to the Prison Service in England and Wales. The working party's Report — *New Directions in Prison Design*[7] — was published in December 1985. The Prison Department's current building programme gives priority to the need to relieve over-crowding in the local prisons and remand centres, and the Department has at present no plans for additional high security prisons after the construction of Full Sutton (which will open in 1987). It is assessing the merits of 'new generation' designs for local prison projects in the forward building programme. When Full Sutton is open and there has been further experience of special units, the Department will consider the possible implications of the 'new generation' designs for long-term maximum security prisons.

---

7.   HMSO, 1985

2
The Research and Advisory Group's Views on the Special Unit Strategy

Method of Working

29. Since our creation in November 1984 we have met on twenty-one occasions at Prison Department Headquarters. In addition, we have made visits to HMP Parkhurst; D Hall and the Hospital Annexe at HMP Wormwood Scrubs; HMP Barlinnie (including the Special Unit); and Park Lane Special Hospital. Some of our members also visited HMP Wakefield, Broadmoor Special Hospital, the Glenthorne Youth Treatment Centre and Aycliffe School, Co Durham. We also spent a very useful day with officials and Governors from the Scottish Home and Health Department discussing the Scottish experience of small units. We are extremely grateful to all those who have given up their time to help us in the course of these visits.

30. In addition we participated in the 18th Cropwood Conference which was organised by the Cambridge Institute of Criminology in March 1986 on the subject of long-term imprisonment. This Conference, which was attended by a mixture of academics and Prison Department officials and governors, provided a useful forum for discussion of some of the issues raised by the CRC Report.[8]

31. The remainder of this Report sets out our advice to the Prison Department on the development of the special units and on the establishment of a related research programme.

The Need for Special Units

32. Three basic assumptions underlie the CRC's recommendations for special units. In summary these are first, that at any one time there exists an identifiable group of long-term prisoners who present serious control problems in the environment in which they are held at that time; second, that the best way to manage these prisoners is to remove them from the dispersal prisons and to hold them instead in small special units; and third, that the

---

8.   The papers presented to the Cropwood Conference are to be published under the title *Problems of Long-Term Imprisonment* (ed. A E Bottoms and R Light), Gower, 1987.

facility provided by the special units will have the effect of reducing the number of serious control problems in the long-term prisons.

The identification of 'difficult prisoners'

33. As far as the first assumption is concerned, we should place on record here that we take the view (as did the CRC) that prisoners present control problems for many different reasons. Difficult prison behaviour is a function of many factors in addition to the prisoner's own character; these factors can include, on occasion, inappropriate prison regimes or mistaken handling of prisoners by staff. Except perhaps in the case of those prisoners whose behaviour is the product of mental disturbance or abnormality, all our experience suggests that most 'troublesome prisoners' present control problems only at particular times or in particular contexts.

34. We began our work by commissioning research by the Prison Department Directorate of Psychological Studies designed to test whether or not it was possible to identify this hypothetical group of prisoners. An account of the research methods employed and of the progress that has been made so far is given in Annex C. Although this work is still continuing, some tentative conclusions can be drawn from it:

(i) on the one hand, there is considerable disagreement between different sources within the prison system about which long-term prisoners can be described as 'difficult';

(ii) on the other hand, taken together, the prisoners[9] described as 'difficult' by the various sources differ significantly from the normal long-term prison population on a number of variables (including the score on a modified version of the US National Institute of Corrections' custody rating scale, and the number of transfers within the prison system on the current sentence).

35. This research therefore appears to suggest that some long-term prisoners *are* more difficult than others, and that their difficult behaviour is not simply a matter of reaction to a particular environment. Nevertheless, the lack of agreement between the sources of referral emphasises the fact that prisoners may behave very differently in different environments and at different points in their sentence.

The alternative offered by small units

36. As far as the second assumption is concerned, the question of whether small units will in fact be more successful in managing prisoners who have presented serious control problems in the long-term prisons is, in principle, an

---

9. A total of 226 and 127 'difficult' prisoners were identified by various sources in the prison system in two successive trawls. Full details of the trawls and the methods employed are given in Annex C.

empirical one to which we hope some answers will be produced by the evaluation of the special units in operation.

37. We accept that the open regime and large populations of the dispersal prisons do make them vulnerable to disorder and also that there are certain prisoners at certain times with whom the dispersals find they cannot cope. The only alternative to normal dispersal life for the majority of these prisoners at present is segregation either in their own establishment or elsewhere. Although segregation is generally seen by prisoners and others as a punitive measure, a short period of segregation need not always be a harmful or purely negative experience. Staff in segregation units are encouraged to spend time talking to prisoners in an effort to help them come to terms with their difficulties in normal location, and a short period of segregation can provide a welcome relief from the pressures of every day prison life or the opportunity for a necessary period of reflection.

38. We believe, however, that *long* periods of segregation actually reduce the likelihood that the prisoner concerned will subsequently be willing or able to cope with normal prison life. We recognise that there is an extremely small number of long-term prisoners who have proved themselves to be exceptionally dangerous (that is, those who have killed in custody and who present a real and continuing threat that they will kill again) and that where these prisoners are concerned long-term segregation may be the only means of ensuring the safety of staff and other inmates.[10] Such prisoners are, however, exceptional and, like the CRC, we reject long-term segregation as an acceptable or effective answer to the problems posed by the overwhelming majority of troublesome prisoners. Apart from the ethical considerations, experience suggests that long-term segregation does not in fact provide a solution to control problems. To quote the CRC:

> 'Many of the prisoners who are unsuited to normal long-term prison life are violent, aggressive men with a very low tolerance threshold. Locking such men up in a confined space for long periods only increases their frustration ... Although segregation removes most of the opportunities for disruptive behaviour, it does nothing to help a prisoner resolve the problems which may lie at the root of [his] failure to cope with the pressures of normal prison life. It is not, therefore, surprising that many of the most disruptive men present serious control problems again almost as soon as they are returned to normal location. Once this pattern develops it may become increasingly difficult to contemplate ever returning the prisoner to normal prison conditions.'

(CRC Report, paragraphs 50 and 67)

---

10. The High Security Cell Unit at Wakefield Prison was created in 1983 in order to provide both a high degree of protection for staff and other inmates and a better quality of life than can be offered in a segregation unit for such exceptionally dangerous prisoners. The Unit has accommodation for two inmates. Each cell is slightly larger than usual and has an adjoining separate small room containing a hand basin, WC and shower. In addition to the external windows, each cell has a glazed opening which overlooks a common area between the cells which contains a television set and seating for visitors. The prisoners in the Unit may communicate with each other, with staff and with visitors but have no physical contact with other prisoners.

39. Small units seem to us to offer a realistic and positive alternative to long-term segregation for these very troublesome prisoners. At the most basic level they will serve the primary need which is the removal of these prisoners from the long-term prisons. And, by definition, they will not offer the scope for large scale disruption that exists in the dispersals. In addition, if the small inmate population is also accompanied by a relatively high ratio of staff (including specialists) to inmates, there will be more opportunities in a small unit for staff and prisoners to get to know each other. Moreover, the number of inmate/inmate relationships that staff will be able to observe and influence in a small unit will obviously be greater than it would be in a large wing (even if the staff/inmate ratio were the same in both). Taking these factors together, we would expect small units to provide an environment in which staff can exercise more effective supervision as well as becoming more closely involved with prisoners than is possible in a normal large dispersal prison wing, and in which inmates can receive more individual attention and support.

The effect on the long-term system

40. The third of the CRC's assumptions, namely, that the small units would contribute to a reduction in control problems in the long-term prisons, is also — in theory at least — empirically testable. It will not be a simple matter to research its validity, however: prisons are complex social institutions which are subject to many different influences whose effects cannot be easily distinguished and attributed. Nevertheless, we consider that an attempt should be made to evaluate the effect that the existence of the units has both on the level of control incidents in the long-term prison system and — just as importantly — on the extent to which staff and inmates in the long-term prisons feel safe and confident. And one very obvious measure of the units' success will be whether, by removing the most persistently disruptive long-term prisoners, they make it possible in due course to reduce the number of dispersal prisons.

General principles

41. Before considering in detail the types of regimes that the units should offer, we arrived through discussion at a number of general principles which we consider should underlie the special unit strategy. These principles are discussed in paragraphs 42 to 57 below.

Centrally planned and complementary regimes

42. We agree with the CRC that it is very important that the different units should complement each other and should not simply be an ad hoc collection of aims and regimes. We, therefore, consider it essential that the regime brief of each unit should be laid down centrally, in accordance with a centrally planned strategy for the development of the special units system. We do not, however, consider that it would be either sensible or practicable to stipulate every detail of the units' regimes in advance from the centre. Factors such as the traditions of the host prison, the nature of the accommodation and the

personalities of staff and inmates will inevitably shape the character of each of the units as they develop. It will, moreover, be essential not to stifle local initiative and innovation if local management and staff are to feel genuinely involved in and committed to the units' objectives. We, therefore, consider that the details of each unit's regime should be drawn up by local management, within the framework of the policy laid down by the centre, in consultation with the staff who will actually work in the units. The development of each unit should then be centrally overseen and monitored to ensure that it remains consistent with the defined regime objectives.

No unit of last resort

43. Although we consider that the regimes of individual units should be complementary, we do not propose that they should be related in any simplistic, progressive manner that would identify one of the units as the 'end of the road'. This is consistent with the CRC's view that none of the units should be regarded as a place of last resort. A last resort unit would quickly fill up with the most difficult prisoners in the system, many of whom would feel that, having reached the end of the road, they no longer had anything to lose by disruptive behaviour. It would be difficult to operate a positive or supportive regime in such a unit.

Non-punitive in purpose

44. We totally endorse the CRC's unequivocal statement that the special units should not be punitive in purpose. The units should not be a further stage in the process of punishment and prisoners should not be allocated to them as a punishment for misbehaviour. The units should offer an alternative environment in which prisoners will have the opportunity to find new ways of coping with imprisonment and relating to staff.

45. The implication of this is that conditions in the units should so far as possible resemble those in normal long-term prisons: that is, the range of permitted privileges and possessions should be similar to those allowed in dispersal prisons; a full programme of constructive activities (including work, education, PE and recreation in association) should be available; and inmates should spend the majority of the day out of their cell.

46. It may be helpful to say something more here about time out of cell. We recognise that the first priority of each unit must be to create an environment in which staff and inmates can feel safe. In order to achieve this it may be necessary in certain circumstances to impose some resrictions on prisoners' freedom of movement (for example, to prohibit association in cells or to limit the number of rooms which are open to prisoners at any particular time). And we recognise that from time to time it will be necessary to segregate individual inmates either on punishment or for reasons of good order and discipline when they pose an unacceptable threat to staff or other prisoners or the stability of the unit. But, given these provisos and safeguards, we believe that it should be

an essential feature of all the units to give all prisoners the opportunity to spend the majority of the day out of their cells in association engaged in purposeful activity.

The relationship between special units and segregation units

47.   The segregation units in the long-term prisons and the CI 10/74 provision (described in paragraph 15 above) will not become redundant with the introduction of special units. The facility they provide for dealing quickly and simply with immediate or short-term control problems will still be needed. What the special units will do, however, will be to extend the options available for managing *persistently* troublesome prisoners and we believe that this will have implications for the use of segregation units.

48.   At present, as we have said, the only alternative to the normal prison wing is a segregation unit or — in a minority of cases — a prison hospital. This means that many prisoners who present serious behavioural problems oscillate constantly between normal location and segregation. As the CRC pointed out, prisoners in this position may feel considerable anger or anxiety about their situation and this can in turn exacerbate their behavioural problems. Once this pattern of misbehaviour-segregation-frustration-misbehaviour-segregation has developed it can be extremely difficult to break it; the periods of segregation are likely to become longer and the periods on normal location to become shorter and more infrequent. The special units will provide an opportunity to bring this destructive cycle to a halt. They will provide a half-way house where prisoners who are either unwilling or unable to cope with normal prison life may be able to develop new patterns of behaviour. Once the units are established, therefore, the option will always exist to transfer prisoners in segregation to a special unit whenever they are ready or able to take advantage of it. During 1984 (the last year for which figures are available) there were 57 inmates who spent at least three months in continuous segregation and a further 22 who spent at least six months in continuous segregation. We would expect to see a significant reduction in this number when the special units are in operation. We would also expect to see some reduction in the use of CI 10/74 (which was employed on 164 occasions during 1985).

Voluntary participation in activities

49.   As we said in paragraph 45 above, we regard it as very important that all the units should provide a full and varied programme of constructive activities and should give inmates the opportunity to spend the majority of the day out of their cells. In general we take the view, however, that the activities provided should not be compulsory, but rather that prisoners should be able to choose not to take part in any activity (although we recognise that sometimes the only alternative will be for a prisoner to remain in his cell for that period).

50.   We would expect that many of the inmates selected for the units will have strong negative attitudes towards staff. If the units are to facilitate the

15

development of constructive staff/inmate relationships, we believe that it will be essential to plan their regimes in ways that reduce the scope for conflict between staff and inmates. It will never be possible to eliminate conflict in the units but we believe that every effort should be made to reduce the occasions for petty and unnecessary friction between staff and inmates. Removing the compulsion on inmates to participate in activities is one way of doing this.

The importance of staff

51. It would be possible to establish special units in which staff deliberately maintain a distance between themselves and inmates (as was the case in the Control Unit[11] which existed at Wakefield from 1974–75). We do not believe, however, that this would be a constructive way forward. Our special units strategy is an attempt to create situations where prisoners will be able to take stock of their behaviour and may be encouraged to find ways of modifying it. We think that this is most likely to be achieved in a positive and supportive environment where there is a high degree of staff involvement with prisoners. Indeed, we believe that the maintenance of control in the units will in fact be critically dependent upon the interpersonal skills of staff, and particularly of the uniformed staff[12]. Small units may offer different ways of optimising the skills of the prison officer in his dealings with particularly difficult prisoners, and this has been an important element in our thinking.

52. It follows from this that we believe that an essential feature of all the units should be the creation of working and managerial structures that will facilitate and encourage close staff involvement with the inmates. A 'personal officer' scheme (whereby an individual officer is allocated responsibility for working closely with a particular inmate) will probably be found to be one of the best means of achieving this. Staff continuity is also a primary condition for the creation of an atmosphere in which close staff/prisoner relationships can develop and we believe that continuity will need to be achieved by appointing staff to work in the special units for a minimum period of, say, two years. Staff training will also be important. We are, therefore, glad to note

---

11. The Control Unit was established at Wakefield in 1974 following the Report of the Home Office Working Party on Dispersal and Control. The regime was divided into two 'stages' each lasting 90 days. At stage one the prisoner did not associate with other prisoners except for one hour's exercise a day. At stage two the prisoner was allowed to associate during work, leisure and educational activities. At the end of the 180 days the prisoner qualified for a return to normal location if he had demonstrated 'sustained good behaviour and constructive effort in the unit'. If at either stage he refused to work or attempted to cause trouble he was required to start the stage again and complete a further continuous period of 90 days good behaviour.

The CRC made it absolutely clear that the Special Units they were advocating would not operate the same kind of regime as the Control Unit. We welcome the fact that both the previous and present Home Secretaries have also stated categorically that there will be no return to the kind of regime which the Control Unit operated.

12. The references to staff in this Report are couched in terms of the existing grade structure. We recognise, however, that the distinction between governor grades and prison officer grades would disappear with the introduction of the 'Fresh Start' proposals (which were published in July and November 1986).

that the Department has found it possible to assign resources to ensure that at least one week's special residential training (concentrating upon interpersonal skills) will be provided for all unit staff.

53.   We should like to see each unit headed by a governor grade whose deputy would be the senior member of the prison officer grades in the unit.[13] The governor in charge of the unit should in our view already have some years' experience in more than one establishment. The governor in charge and the prison officer grades should be supported by specialist staff and all staff in the unit (governor, prison officers and specialists) will need to work closely together as part of an inter-disciplinary team.

Length of stay

54.   We have concluded that it is not possible at present to specify how long prisoners should remain in the units. We assume that for some prisoners the units' role will be to see them through a critical period when they are having difficulty reconciling themselves to normal prison conditions and then to return them to a normal long-term prison again after a matter of months. Other prisoners, who have very great difficulties in coping with life in a normal prison or who persistently present serious control problems, may need to remain in one or other of the special units for several years. Relevant factors in determining length of stay will be the degree to which the units are able to achieve changes in prisoners' attitudes, social skills and behaviour, and the judgement that is made about a prisoner's likely behaviour on return to normal location.

55.   If there proves to be a large number of prisoners in the units whose behaviour does not change and who continue to be considered unsuited to normal location, a decision will need to be taken as to whether the units' role should be to provide a long-term alternative to normal location (in which case more units might need to be created) or a short-term alternative (in which case prisoners whose behaviour has not changed in the units might be moved out in order to make way for newcomers). Without more experience of the units in operation it is too early to make a judgement about which approach would make the best use of the units — or, indeed, to know whether the question will ever arise in practice.

Openness and accountability

56.   We share the CRC's view that it is essential that the Prison Service should be completely open about the establishment of the units and the way they operate. It is our view, for example, that the aims and objectives of individual units should be available to all those (including inmates) who wish to see them. We recognise that in the early stages of their development it will not be helpful for units to be exposed to too much outside attention, since both staff and

---

13.   See footnote 12 to paragraph 51.

inmates will require time to adjust to their new environment and the different demands made upon them. Once the units are established, however, we believe that the presumption should be in favour of permitting visits by outside organisations and individuals.

57.   Structures of accountability also seem to us to be particularly important in this context. We believe that — as is already the case with the use of segregation — the operation of the special units should be made the object of special care by governors and Regional Directors in exercising their role as line managers, and should receive particular attention from Boards of Visitors. And in due course we hope that HM Inspectorate of Prisons will also pay close attention to the operation of the units in the course of its regular programme of inspections of establishments. We also regard it as important in this context that outside organisations should be involved in the research into the special units and that the results of such research should be published.

Sites

58.   We have naturally given some thought to the types of sites that would be appropriate for the establishment of special units. We recognised very early in our work that, since the existing prison plant does not readily lend itself to conversion into self-contained units, the number of potential special unit sites around the system is very limited indeed. We have, therefore, confined ourselves to making some general observations about special unit accommodation.

59.   As regards *host prisons*, the CRC took the view that the units might be sited either 'in local prisons or in long-term prisons, provided that they are physically discrete and offer an overall level of security suited to the prisoners they contain'[14] and we note that the Department is contemplating some units in dispersals and others in local prisons. We do not think that there is sufficient evidence at present for us to say that one kind of host prison will necessarily provide a more appropriate environment for a special unit than another.

60.   Wherever special units are sited, we think that it will be important for them to be seen as an integral part of the host prison and we hope that it will be possible for most of their staff to be drawn from the host prison. Otherwise there is a danger that misunderstandings and antagonisms will develop between those working in the main prison and those in the unit. This would be bound to put unnecessary stress on staff in the unit.

61.   All prisons vary in their style and structure. If the special unit staff are drawn from the main prison we consider it almost inevitable that the units will, initially at least, reflect some of the character and traditions of the establishments in which they are situated. This suggests that, in deciding what regime to establish where, one of the factors that it will make sense to take into

---

14.   CRC Report, paragraph 54.

account will be the nature of the various host prisons and the skills and experience of their staff. We do not, however, preclude the possibility of establishment some units whose regimes are very different in kind from that of their host prison. The establishment of the special units is an experimental situation and we believe that an important opportunity will have been missed if no attempt is made to break new ground in regime terms in some of the units. The experience of the Barlinnie Special Unit suggests that it is possible to establish a completely new kind of regime even in a local prison setting if the mangement and staff in the unit are involved in the project from an early stage.[15]

62. With regard to *security* we accept the view of the CRC and the Department's professional advisers that security considerations do not demand that all the units have perimeter security of the standard required at Category B dispersal prisons. With regard to *discreteness*, we do not interpret the CRC as saying that the units should be housed in completely separate buildings, but rather that they should be managerially separate. We take the view that it is seldom, if ever, possible to hold a group of prisoners in such a way that they are completely unable to communicate with other prisoners within the same perimeter wall. While, therefore, it will always be necessary to consider very carefully what effect a potential unit might have upon the host prison, we think that it will generally be sufficient for special units to be housed in self-contained accommodation in which a full range of activities can take place. The units' inmates need not therefore leave the unit (except when being transferred to the hospital or segregation unit) unless local management considers it safe and desirable for them to do so.

63. We do not feel able at present to stipulate a specific *size* (in terms of inmate numbers) for special units since there has been very little research into

---

15.   The Barlinnie Special Unit has been in existence since February 1973. It is located in the former women's block within the perimeter of Barlinnie Prison, a local prison in Glasgow.

The Unit holds a maximum of 8 long-term prisoners who will typically be potentially violent, volatile and intelligent. All staff, other than the Governor, are volunteers.

The Unit operates as a social community. Formal community meetings of inmates and staff are held each week and all internal matters (other than security and staffing issues) are open to discussion at these meetings.

There is no formalised system of punishment in the Unit. When internally agreed procedures are broken the prisoner has to explain his actions to the other members of the community. There is no structured programme of work. Prisoners are encouraged to develop individual interests in art, sculpture, woodwork, education, PE or hobbies. Prisoners' correspondence is not censored (except during an early supervised period when a prisoner first enters the unit). There is no restriction on the number of visits prisoners may receive. A wide range of people visit the unit, all of whom must be approved by the community. After the initial supervised period visits may be taken unsupervised in cells.

Successive governments have confirmed their view that the Unit forms an integral part of the Scottish prison system. The Unit also has the whole-hearted support of the Scottish Prison Officers' Association.

Two accounts of the development and operation of the Barlinnie Special Unit are given in Chapters 11 and 12 of the Cropwood Conference publication (see the footnote to paragraph 30 above).

this question either in the prison system or in other related residential contexts. All that we can, therefore, say at this stage is that there should be a variety of unit sizes, and that units should be as spacious as possible (both because adequate space for out of cell activities is essential, and because there is some reason to believe that a sense of personal space may be particularly important to many of the individuals who will be held in the units).

64. Experience suggests that in practice it will be found that there is an ideal size for each unit, beyond which control problems will multiply and/or the regime and the nature of staff/inmate interactions will change significantly. This 'ideal size' will almost certainly differ from unit to unit and will be likely to be influenced by the unit's regime as much as by its physical layout. The implication of this is that it will be important not to be too dogmatic in advance about the maximum population which each unit should hold, but to keep the size under review as the units develop and be ready to make changes as necessary.

Special unit regimes

65. In considering what regimes should be established in the special units we have begun by acknowledging that very little is known in a verifiable scientific sense about either the problem behaviour of individual prisoners and the psychology that underpins that behaviour, or the contexts in which problem behaviours occur and the complex interactions that give rise to such behaviours. Indeed, there has been very little detailed descriptive research into the ways in which staff, prisoners and regimes interact in our prisons generally. It is therefore not possible to predict with confidence that a particular kind of regime will 'work' with a particular 'type' of problem prisoner. Given the present state of knowledge, it seems sensible to proceed with a pragmatic strategy for developing special units that combines the following elements:

(i)   the utilisation of whatever relevant experience and resources already exist within the prison system;

(ii)   a systematic programme of monitoring and research evaluation; and

(iii)   a commitment to feed both the results of research and the benefits of the experience of implementing the special unit strategy back into the long-term prison system generally.

The utilisation of existing experience

66. As we have said, the normal day to day employment of interpersonal skills by uniformed officers is a critical factor in the maintenance of control in prisons. This is particularly the case in long-term prisons where inmates are free to mix in large groups within an open regime. When these relationships persistently fail or break down for one reason or another with a

20

particular inmate there are essentially three responses available to prison governors in dealing with that prisoner: *transfer, segregation* and *specialist assistance.*

67. The rationale behind the strategy of *transfer* is two-fold. First, it provides relief for the staff (and other inmates) who have to cope with a troublesome prisoner. Second, using the knowledge that prisoners behave differently in different contexts, transfer involves the deliberate removal of a prisoner from one context and his placement in a different context in which it is hoped he will behave better.

68. *Segregation* is a particular form of transfer which involves the removal of a prisoner from association with other prisoners. Segregation will generally be in a part of the establishment set aside for that purpose, and will inevitably involve some loss of privileges and opportunities provided in the ordinary regime (although we note that prison governors are encouraged to limit this additional deprivation if practicable, especially if a prisoner is segregated for a lengthy period of time).

69. *Specialist assistance* (which may be used alone or in conjunction with transfer or segregation) involves the application of the knowledge or skills of a particular specialist discipline such as psychiatry or psychology in an attempt to assist with the modification or control of prisoners' behaviour.

70. The special units strategy that we envisage will be a development of the transfer response since it will involve the deliberate transfer of a prisoner from his immediate location (which may be a segregation unit, a prison hospital or the open regime characteristic of a dispersal prison) to a different environment. It is explicitly not a strategy of segregation since, as we have said, we consider it important that all the units should offer prisoners the opportunity to spend the majority of the day out of their cell in association with other prisoners. The special units will thus be quite different from existing segregation units and from the Control Unit[16] which existed at Wakefield from 1974–75.

71. We intend that the special units strategy should also utilise existing specialist knowledge and skills and thus build, as systematically as possible, on what is known and what can be learned about what different kinds of specialisms can contribute.

Specialist assistance

72. It seems to us that there are three main forms that specialist assistance could take in the special units:

(i) direct availability of specialist services to the inmates;

(ii) assistance to management and staff;

---

16. See the footnote 11 to paragraph 51 above.

(iii)   the use of concepts associated with a particular specialism to inform the principles and practices of a unit's regime.

Any particular unit might draw upon the same specialism for each of these three types of assistance or a different specialism might be involved in each. Types (i) and (ii) would generally be performed by specialist staff directly employed in the units; in the case of type (iii) this might not be the case. All three types of assitance need not necessarily be provided in every unit.

73.   The types of specialist assistance most frequently called upon at present by dispersal governors in their attempts to deal with the control problems posed by long-term prisoners are referral to a psychiatrist and referral to a psychologist. Special unit regimes drawing upon both these specialisms can be readily envisaged.

74.   An example of a special unit regime which drew upon *psychiatry* to perform all the roles described in paragraph 72 above was the unit that existed at C Wing, Parkhurst from 1970–1979. This unit provided a facility for prisoners who had a history of mental disturbance or abnormality and who had also demonstrated behavioural problems. The management team included a psychiatrist and the uniformed staff were a mixture of discipline and hospital officers. Specific psychiatric assistance (in the form of drug treatment or psychiatric counselling sessions) was available for those prisoners who wished to receive it. The psychiatrist attached to the unit gave advice to management and staff on the handling of all the unit's inmates, and psychiatric knowledge informed many of the principles and practices of the unit's regime.

75.   A regime drawing upon the concept of *psychological assistance* might be similar in many respects to one drawing upon psychiatric assistance. It would differ primarily in the extent to which prospective inmates had current or previous psychiatric histories. First, a range of professional services (such as social skills training, anger control programmes and individual counselling and group work) designed to deal with problematic behaviour could be made available to those inmates who wished to take advantage of them. Second, psychological assessment of individual inmates might be used to advise staff about the way in which they should respond to particular individuals. And, third, psychological concepts might be used to inform the design and organisation of the regime generally.

76.   In addition to regimes drawing upon the relatively familiar assistance that may be provided by psychiatrists and psychologists, it is possible to envisage regimes which would draw at least in part upon the skills and knowledge of other specialisms. Such specialisms may be of particular relevance in developing ideas that will inform the principles and practices of a unit's regime (the third type of specialist assistance identified in paragraph 72 above); examples of relevant fields of knowledge in this respect would be management science, education and sociology.

77.   One particular line of thought, derived from sociological and social psychological research and theory, seems to us to be especially worth

developing. As we have already said, experience suggests that most trouble-some prisoners present control problems only at particular times or in particular contexts (paragraph 33 above). In the course of their work prison staff naturally develop views about the best approach to adopt with individual prisoners and about what kind of prisoner might fit in well (or badly) at a particular establishment or in a particular wing or workshop within a prison. Underlying these views is an intuitive understanding that the ways in which individual staff and prisoners relate to each other and the social situations within which they come into contact can make it easier or more difficult for prisoners and staff to co-exist in a peaceable way.

78. Perhaps not surprisingly, there is at present no research that adequately tests the validity of these understandings. The general literature on the sociology of imprisonment does, however, suggest that the way in which staff and inmates interact can make a major contribution to the maintenance of control, and, equally, that disorder can result when a situation is misread or an inappropriate response is given.

79. We recommend below (see Section 3) a programme of research that is intended inter alia to develop a more refined, sociological understanding of the ways in which interactions between prisoners and the prison diminish or exacerbate problem behaviour by prisoners. We should like to see the emerging results of this research used systematically in the special unit system (both in the selection and allocation process, and in some aspects of regime development) — preferably in a careful synthesis with, first, relevant prior research in this country and elsewhere (limited in quantity though this is[17]), and, secondly, with existing theoretical work in sociology, notably on the concept of social control[18].

80. The kind of sociological insight developed through this process could also be applied to the construction of a special unit regime which treats the interaction between staff and inmates as being (for some inmates at least) a central issue in the genesis or avoidance of problem behaviour by prisoners, and which therefore deliberately requires participative discussion about such interactions as a focal point of its activities[19].

Other characteristics of regimes

81. The nature, range and extent of its specialist assistance will be an important element that distinguishes one special unit regime from another.

---

17. See for example *Albany: Birth of a Prison, End of an Era*, by Roy D King and Kenneth Elliott, Routledge 1978. We hope that the literature survey on control in prisons by the Home Office Research and Planning Unit (see Annex D) will provide a comprehensive guide to the relevant research.

18. See the volume arising from the Cropwood Conference (paragraph 30 above), especially the introduction and the chapter by Peter Young.

19. Although the Barlinnie Special Unit has not been formally researched, it seems to us (from the published accounts of the Unit's operation, and from discussions we have held with those familiar with the Unit) that this Unit's apparent success in dealing with some control problem prisoners derives, at least in part, from its taking an approach of this kind. The Barlinne Special Unit has not, however, explicitly used sociological theory and research in its development.

Characterising a special unit by a particular type of specialist involvement will not, however, provide a complete description of that unit's regime: for example, a regime based upon behaviourist principles and a regime that makes use of clinical psychologists would both draw their inspiration from psychological concepts, but might differ in almost every other respect.

Structure

82.   We have identified two further elements which in our view distinguish other important differences between regimes. The first of these is the *degree of structure* built into the regime. By this we mean the degree to which prisoners are free to make choices about their use of time and space. The degree of structure present in regimes varies considerably from one type of establishment to another throughout the prison system. Local prisons, for example, are characteristed by a highly structured regime where particular pre-determined activities take place at particular pre-determined times and in particular pre-determined places. By comparison, prisoners in a dispersal prison have a much greater degree of choice about how and where they spend their time. Even this, however, is not as loosely structured as the regime of the Barlinnie Special Unit where, with the exception of attendance at community meetings (which is compulsory), inmates are free to occupy themselves in any activity they wish, in any part of the unit or at any time of the day. It is clear from these examples that there are significant differences between a regime that may be characterised as highly structured and one that may be characterised as loosely structured. It will, therefore, be important that those who will be designing individual unit regimes are given clear guidance in advance about the degree of structure that is required.

Staff/inmate interactions

83.   A further element that seems to us to characterise regimes is the *nature of the interactions between staff and inmates*. By this we mean three things:

(i)   the amount of time staff and inmates spend talking to each other (whatever the subject);

(ii)   the degree to which inmates participate in the running of the establishment or unit; and

(iii)   the degree to which inmates are encouraged to involve themselves in finding ways of modifying their behaviour.

84.   As we said in paragraph 52 above, we believe that the creation of working structures (such as personal officer scheme) that facilitate and encourage close staff involvement with prisoners should be an essential feature of all the special units. We do not recommend therefore that the special unit regimes should be differentiated from each other by the amount of contact and

discussion that takes place between staff and inmates. We do expect, however, that there will be significant differences in this respect between the special units and the average segregation unit.

85.   The degree to which prisoners participate in decisions about the running of the unit is, however, an area in which the special units might usefully differ in order to provide a variety of regimes within the special unit system. In a local prison there is little scope for inmates to have any say in the way in which the establishment and its routines are organised. In the Barlinnie Special Unit on the other hand most of the unit's internal matters (including practical details such as the cooking arrangements; the resolution of disputes between two inmates or between an inmate and a member of staff; and the imposition of appropriate sanctions when a prisoner breaks the community's rules) are decided at regular community meetings at which attendance is compulsory for management, staff and prisoners. It is possible to envisage a wide range of interim positions between these two extremes.

86.   There will be certain similarities between all the units with regard to the third area — the extent to which prisoners are actively involved in finding ways of modifying their own behaviour. In all the units, as in any prison situation, there will be occasions when it is appropriate to regard prisoners as autonomous individuals who are in control of their behaviour and therefore able to participate in finding a solution to the problems they present. There will be other occasions when it will be more appropriate to impose a staff-determined reponse to problem behaviour. Having said that, we nevertheless believe that there will still be significant differences between the units in this respect since certain kinds of specialist intervention and certain kinds of structure will obviously offer more or less scope than others for involving prisoners directly in attempts to modify their problem behaviour.

The numbers and types of units

87.   We should like to see the establishment of a range of special units each characterised by differing kinds of specialist assistance, and further characterised by varying degrees of structure and by the nature of the staff/inmate interactions which they facilitate and encourage (particularly by the extent to which inmates are involved in the running of the unit and/or in finding ways of modifying their own problem behaviour). Four or five different regimes should provide sufficient variety in the first instance. Further units could then be added in the light of what evaluation revealed about which kinds of regimes 'work' best.

88.   As we have said, we have rejected the concept of a progressive relationship between the units. We have therefore concluded that there is at present no theoretical basis for electing to establish one kind of regime before or after another. We recognise that the special units are something of a new departure for the Prison Service. If the system is to have credibility in the eyes of governors and staff it seems sensible, at least in the early days of its

development, to try to take account of what the field perceive their needs to be. It will be essential, however, that these expectations are not permitted to produce unacceptable distortions of the special units strategy.

89.   It is not possible to predict exactly how many special unit places will be required. The research carried out for us by the Prison Department Directorate of Psychological Studies (described in Annex C) found that 226 and 127 long-term prisoners were identified as 'troublesome' by various sources in the prison system in two successive trawls. As we explain below, however, we do not believe that it would be wise to interpret this research as suggesting that 226 special unit places are required.

90.   It has never been the intention that the special units would relieve the long-term prisons of *all* troublesome prisoners. In the nature of things long-term prisons will always contain a proportion of difficult inmates and their staff will always need to possess the skills to deal with such prisoners. This will still be the case when the units are in operation. What the special units are intended to do is to relieve the long-term establishments of prisoners who are *seriously* or *persistently* troublesome. The fact that over 200 prisoners have been identified as 'troublesome' at a particular time cannot be read as necessarily implying that they all present such serious or persistent control problems in a variety of environments as to warrant their transfer to a special unit. The segregation units and the CI 10/74 facility will continue to be the most appropriate responses to prisoners who present short-term, immediate or relatively minor control problems.

91.   Moreover, although some of the prisoners who are transferred to special units may need to remain there for long periods, the hope is that others will return to normal location after a relatively short time. We would, therefore, expect to find that a single unit place may be occupied by more than one inmate over the course of a year.

92.   Finally, of the various sources used to identify 'troublesome' prisoners in the course of the research referred to above, it is prison governors who have the most direct personal contact with the prisoners concerned. It is also they who will be responsible in practice for nominating prisoners for special units. This suggests that the number of inmates identified as 'troublesome' by prison governors — 108 — is likely to be the best guide to the numbers that may actually be nominated for special unit places.

93.   For all these reasons we think that it will be sensible to aim to establish no more than 100 special unit places in the first instance and to create more only if the need is subsequently shown to exist.

3
Research Needs Identified by the Research and Advisory Group

94. We regard the establishment of a related research programme as an integral part of our special units strategy. Such a programme will need to include research into the maintenance of control in the long-term prison system generally, as well as the systematic monitoring and evaluation of the special units themselves. The lessons gleaned from this research will, of course, need to be fed back into the development of the special unit strategy. We hope very much that they will also be fed back into the prison system as a whole. We describe below the kind of research programme that we have recommended the Department should fund.

95. First, we have recommended that it would be valuable to have a literature survey of those *aspects of prison regimes that appear to assist or militate against the maintenance of control* (including the composition of an establishment's population).

96. Second, we have recommended that an examination should be commissioned into *the nature of control problems among long-term prisoners and their emergence*, including a study of the circumstances in which prisoners are transferred from normal location. We have also suggested that there might be value in a study of *regional and institutional variations in the occurrence of control incidents* and in the emergence of people presenting control problems.

97. Third, we have recommended that a short study should be conducted of the *special security units* in the prison system. The intention would be, while recognising that these units are for prisoners for whom especially high security is considered necessary, to pay particular attention to aspects that might be useful in connection with the establishment of the special units for those presenting control problems.

98. Fourth, with regard to *the special units* themselves, we have recommended that:

(i)   a descriptive and evaluative account should be prepared of each special unit;

(ii)   an attempt should be made to evaluate the effect that the existence of the units has on the level of control incidents in the long-term prison system; and

(iii) the process of allocating prisoners to the special units should be monitored.

99. Once several special units are in operation and in the light of the findings of the research already commissioned, we intend to consider whether further research might usefully be conducted into the special units. In particular we have in mind:

(a) a comparative evaluation of the regimes of the special units in the context of the special unit system as a whole;

(b) a study of whether the units have any effect on their host prisons;

(c) an attempt to evaluate the effect that the existence of the units has on the feelings of confidence and safety experienced by staff and inmates in the dispersal prisons; and

(d) a study of the units' cost effectiveness in the context of the long-term prison system as a whole.

100. We are also aware that the following areas will be of particular concern to those administering the special units:

(i) the extent to which prisoners allocated to the special units have presented more serious control problems in prison than those who are not referred or allocated to the units;

(ii) whether it is possible to identify in advance those prisoners who will present fewer control problems in special units than in normal prison wings; and

(iii) whether it is possible to identify those prisoners who will present the greatest control problems in special units.

It seems to us that there would be considerable methodological difficulties in conducting research into the second and third of these areas, but we shall be considering at a later stage in our work whether or not these difficulties can be resolved.

101. We have also noted the relevance to our work of a research project being conducted by the University College of North Wales, under the direction of Professor Roy King, with a grant from the Economic and Social Research Council. This project — a study of security, control and humane containment in the prison system of England and Wales — does not concentrate on the long-term prisons, but it includes a dispersal prison among the establishments to be studied and should throw valuable light on the nature of the regime activities of such an establishment. It will also include a study of prisoners' and staff perceptions of the dispersal regime. The dispersal prison regime seems to us a vital area for research and in the light of what we hear in the

future about the progress of this research project, we may consider recommending in due course that the Prison Department commissions a study of its own on this topic.

102. Finally, we should add that at a later stage in our work we shall be considering what recommendations we wish to make to the Prison Department concerning research into other areas identified by the CRC (such as security categorisation, prison design and sentence planning). To date, however, we have concentrated on research specifically related to the special units and the maintenance of control in long-term prisons.

4
The Implementation
of our Advice

103.   The Prison Department has accepted in principle both the general recommendations we have made (see paragraphs 41 to 64) and the specific strategy we have proposed (see paragraphs 65 to 93) in Section Two of this Report. We particularly welcome the knowledge that the Department has accepted our research recommendations (set out in Section Three of this Report) and that the key projects we have proposed are currently in hand or about to be commissioned with funding from the Home Office Research and Planning Unit (see Annex D). In paragraphs 104 to 125 below we describe the steps that have been or are being taken by the Prison Department to implement our advice on the establishment of the special unit system.

Sites

104.   As we said in paragraph 58 above, the number of sites around the prison system that are suitable for conversion to special units is not large. Out of the various sites that were inspected, the Department has now identified the following five that it regards as having good potential:

Site	Maximum No. of places available	Estimated opening date	Comment
Parkhurst, C Wing	26	Opened December 1985	Located in a 19th Century building within a dispersal prison.
Lincoln, Annexe to C Wing	9	May 1987	Located in a 19th Century building within a local prison.
Hull, A Wing	25	March 1988	Located in a post-Second World War building within a local prison with very recent dispersal experience.

Frankland,	10–15	March/April 1989	Adjacent to the prison hospital. Located in accommodation built in the late 1970s within a dispersal prison.
			Currently the subject of a feasibility study.
Milton Keynes	16	1992	Unit to be built within a new local prison (consideration is being given to building both the prison and the unit to 'new generation' designs).

105.   Between them these sites seem to us to offer a satisfactory variety of types of accommodation (ranging from Victorian galleried landings to the possibility of a purpose-built 'new generation' unit), host prison and size. (As we said in paragraph 64, the precise number of prisoners that a particular unit can safely contain is a matter that will need to be kept under review. The figures given above for the maximum number of places at each site are therefore based at present on the advice of practitioners about what will be practicable in each case, and may need to be revised in the light of experience.) Assuming that the Frankland site does become available, these five sites would together provide up to 90 special unit places by 1992. As we said in paragraph 93 above, we consider that this is a sensible number of places to plan for at this stage; five units should also enable a sufficient variety of regimes to be created. In the event of the Frankland site being rejected as unsuitable following the feasibility study, we therefore recommend that the Department should identify an alternative site capable of accommodating 15–20 prisoners.

Regimes

106.   The sites that are either available or likely to become available each have their own strengths and weaknesses. In deciding what kind of regime to establish where, the Prison Department has taken account of factors such as the size and physical structure of the accommodation, the traditions and experience of staff, the nature of the host prison, and proximity to centres of population. The Department has also taken account of what it believes to be the views of dispersal prison governors and staff.

C Wing, Parkhurst

107.   Following the publication of the Control Review Committee Report in July 1984 the then Home Secretary immediately asked that work be set in hand

to open a special unit in C Wing, Parkhurst to be run on similar lines to that of the previous unit there[20]. This unit, which opened in December 1985, includes a psychiatrist as one of the members of its management team and is staffed by a mixture of Hospital Officers and Discipline Officers. It is designed to provide general psychiatric oversight and, where appropriate, individual psychiatric care for prisoners with a history of both troublesome prison behaviour and of psychiatric abnormality or disturbance. Its regime, admission criteria and population at the time of writing are described in Annex E.

108.   In terms of our analysis of the available regime variables, the Parkhurst Unit is characterised by wide-ranging specialist assistance of a psychiatric nature. The psychiatrist attached to the unit provides professional services (from medication to counselling) for those prisoners who are in need of such treatment and who wish to receive it. He also provides advice and guidance to management and staff in their dealings with individual inmates. The regime is 'therapeutic' in nature and psychiatric knowledge and skills therefore underpin many of its principles and practices and the way in which staff interact with inmates generally. A psychologist attached to the unit also provides an important input of specialist assistance by providing counselling and therapy for individual inmates and advice to management and staff.

109.   The regime is also characterised by an intermediate degree of structure. Inmates have a significant degree of choice over how they spend their time but those who do not wish to take part in any of the activities on offer at any particular time will remain locked in their cell. And, in order to minimise the risk of prisoner to prisoner violence and hostage taking, it has been decided that inmates should not be permitted to associate together in their cells, but only on the landings where they can be supervised by staff.

110.   With regard to the nature of the interactions between staff and inmates, the personal officer scheme used in the unit encourages a very high degree of staff involvement with prisoners and helps to avoid problem behaviour. The regime also promotes some opportunities for inmates to become involved in finding ways of modifying their own behaviour (through talking to their personal officer, through counselling sessions with the psychiatrist or psychologist or by taking part if they wish in the regular reviews of their case held by management and staff). Inmates do not participate in the running and organisation of the unit.

The Lincoln Unit

111.   In considering the types of regimes to be established in the units immediately following the Parkhurst Unit the Department has been influenced chiefly by the practical factors referred to in paragraph 106 above. The first site to become available after Parkhurst will be the Annexe to C Wing at

---

20.   For a description of this unit see paragraph 74 above and also paragraphs 60 and 61 of the CRC Report.

Lincoln which offers accommodation for a very small number of prisoners (nine) but relatively good space for out of cell activities. The host prison is a traditional local prison. The Department concluded that the most suitable regime for this unit would be one which used the traditional skills of prison officers in working with small numbers of inmates and which provided as far as possible the range of activities that are normally available for long-term prisoners.

112.   The decision was therefore taken to establish a unit at Lincoln which will be characterised by a higher degree of structure than the Parkhurst Unit. It is intended that a wide range of out of cell activities will be provided in a pre-arranged programme, but that inmates who choose not to take part in the particular activity scheduled for them at a particular time will remain locked in their cell; and, as at the Parkhurst Unit, inmates will not be permitted to associate in their cells.

113.   Again as at the Parkhurst Unit, a personal officer scheme will be used which will facilitate and encourage a high degree of staff involvement with inmates. The personal officer scheme will also offer opportunities for inmates to discuss difficulties with staff and this may enable problem behaviour to be avoided. Inmates will have no say in the running of the unit.

114.   A major feature of the unit's regime will be the utilisation of prison officers' skills in dealing with prisoners and there will be only a very limited amount of specialist assistance — and none directed to the inmates personally. There will however be a psychologist attached to the unit on a part-time basis who will be involved in drawing up the staff training programme and who will provide general support and advice to management and staff.

115.   Local management are now involved in planning the details of the unit's regime and the unit is scheduled to open in May 1987.

The Hull Unit

116.   The next site to become available will be A Wing at Hull. This site is a small wing with galleried landings which offers good space for out of cell activities. The main prison operated as a dispersal from 1969 to February 1986 and A Wing itself will continue to hold long-term prisoners in Categories A and B and will run an open regime of the type customary in dispersals until mid-1987 (when the wing will be emptied so that building work to convert it into a self-contained special unit can begin). This means that staff at Hull have recent experience of handling long-term prisoners in an open regime and the Department has tried to capitalise on this in determining the regime to be established in the unit.

117.   The first unit to be established — C Wing, Parkhurst — caters for a particular sub-set of the disruptive population (ie. those who have a history of mental abnormality) and, although the Lincoln Unit will have no restrictions on admission, it will be able to hold only nine prisoners. In reaching a decision

about the Hull Unit's regime the Department had regard to the fact that, in its view, if the special units system were to have credibility in the eyes of dispersal governors and staff, it would be important for the units to be seen at an early stage to be relieving the dispersal prisons of a broad range of disruptive prisoners. The Department therefore concluded that it would be a mistake to establish a regime in the third unit which, like the Parkhurst Unit, would be suitable only for a narrowly defined range of prisoners. The Department accordingly decided that the Hull Unit's regime should be such as to enable it to take any disruptive prisoners who do not require the kind of psychiatric oversight that C Wing, Parkhurst provides.

118.   A regime is proposed that will be broadly similar in nature to that of a normal dispersal prison in terms of its degree of structure (and therefore less structured than that of the Lincoln Unit). In addition it is intended that the psychologist attached to the unit should develop a range of programmes (including counselling and social learning therapies) for those prisoners who wish to take advantage of them. The regime will, therefore, also be characterised by some specialist assistance of a psychological nature in the form of the availability of professional services to inmates. The psychologist attached to the unit will also play a part in drawing up the staff training programme and will provide support and assistance to management and staff in their dealings with inmates.

119.   As at Parkhurst and Lincoln a personal officer scheme will be used and this should facilitate a high degree of staff involvement with prisoners. The opportunities offered for prisoners to become involved in finding ways of modifying their own problem behaviour (through contact with their personal officer and, if they wish, by taking advantage of the psychologist's services) will be roughly comparable to those at the Parkhurst Unit (and therefore greater than those at the Lincoln Unit). Prisoners will have no say in the running of the unit.

120.   The Department has not yet decided what regimes should be established at the two remaining sites likely to become available — Frankland and Milton Keynes. Our own recommendations on this subject are set out in paragraphs 128 to 133 below.

Allocation

The Special Units Selection Committee

121.   If the special units are to serve the long-term prison system as a whole, it is essential that entry into and out of them is centrally controlled and monitored by a body that is in a position to assess the problems of the system nationally. The Department has established a committee — the Special Units Selection Committee (SUSC) — to perform this function. The Committee is chaired by the Head of P3 Division (who is a member of our Group) and its membership comprises representatives from the relevant Headquarters

Directorates and from the management of the Parkhurst Unit. It is intended that the Committee should in due course be augmented by the governor and the senior uniformed officer[21] of each of the other special units as they come into operation.

Allocation into the units

122.   The details of prisoners who may be special unit candidates are generally referred to SUSC for consideration by the governors of the dispersal prisons or the other training prisons that contain long-termers. It is not, however, uncommon for long-term prisoners to be held outside the long-term system, perhaps for some months and usually in local prisons, if they have presented serious control problems with which the long-term prisons cannot cope. For this reason local prison governors have also been invited to refer the cases of long-term prisoners who have been transferred to them following persistent seriously disruptive behaviour in the long-term system.

123.   Referrals are made on a standard form (attached at Annex F) which seeks information about the inmate's institutional history and behaviour from his Personal Officer, Wing Manager, Medical Officer, Psychologist and Probation Officer as well as the Governor.

124.   SUSC meets approximately every six weeks to consider referrals. At the time of writing C Wing, Parkhurst is the only unit in operation and the Committee's task is, therefore, limited at present to deciding whether or not the cases referred meet the C Wing admission criteria and whether or not the prisoner should also be considered for a transfer to Grendon (which continues to play an important part in the treatment of prisoners with mental disorder, including prisoners who have been troublesome in other establishments). When the other units are in operation the task will be extended to deciding first, whether or not the prisoner should be transferred into the special units system and, then, if so, which of the units is the most suitable for him. As a general rule the Committee would expect prisoners who are selected for the special units to have a history of frequent or long periods in segregation units or prison hospitals and/or a history of frequent transfers between establishments. Once a prisoner has been selected for a particular unit the Committee decides whether he should be transferred immediately or whether he should be placed on a waiting list. The latter course is adopted on those occasions when it is thought that the entry of a particular prisoner at a particular time could place the stability of the unit as a whole in jeopardy.

Allocation out of the units

125.   Prisoners may be removed from a unit temporarily to the host prison's segregation unit (on punishment or under Rule 43 GOAD) or to a local prison for one month under CI 10/74 without reference to SUSC. Any permanent

---

21.   See footnote 12 to paragraph 51 above.

transfer out must, however, be authorised by SUSC. Each prisoner's case is reviewed by SUSC after the first 10 weeks in the unit and thereafter at approximately three to six monthly intervals. On the basis of these reviews, which are considered at the regular meetings, SUSC decides whether or not a prisoner should remain in the unit concerned. If the Committee decides that a transfer is appropriate they will also consider where the prisoner should be transferred to (for example another unit, a normal dispersal prison or a training prison, or, in what we hope will be a few cases, a segregation unit). In this way the Special Units Selection Committee will be responsible for planning the careers of this group of troublesome long-term prisoners.

Our comments

Allocation

126. We are content with the procedures the Prison Department has introduced for the allocation of prisoners into and out of the special units.

Regimes

127. The regimes planned for the first three units — Parkhurst, Lincoln and Hull — will be familiar and readily understood by staff throughout the long-term prison system. As such, they seem to us to represent a sensible start to the implementation of the strategy we have proposed. We have accordingly given our assistance to the drawing up of the outline regime briefs for these three units, although, of course, the final decisions have been taken by the Prison Department.

128. As we have already indicated (paragraph 16), the CRC did not attempt to specify exactly what regimes were needed in the special unit system, but it did say that, in the present state of knowledge, 'what is required . . . is variety of provision and the willingness to innovate and adapt regimes in the light of experience' (CRC Report, paragraph 65; see also paragraph 56 of the CRC Report). We strongly agree with both parts of this comment. Willingness to adapt regimes in the light of experience should be facilitated by the research programme we have recommended, and we have already given one particular example of the way in which such adaptation could take place (paragraph 79). As regards variety, we take the view that if our recommended general strategy for special units is to succeed, and is to conform to the expectations of the CRC, a wider range of regimes than is encompassed by the first three units should be established. We therefore hope that the Prison Department will take the opportunity presented by the remaining two identified sites — Frankland and Milton Keynes — to introduce units of a deliberately different character.

129. We consider that one such unit should be established with *specialist psychological assistance* as a major feature, along the lines set out in paragraph 75 above. This would differ from the Hull regime (which will also incorporate some counselling and social learning programmes) because psychological concepts and programmes would be much more central to the

36

functioning of the unit, which would aim to contribute to the reduction of the prisoners' difficulties by the planned application of psychological principles. The degree of structure appropriate to a unit of this kind would have to be determined in the light of choices made about the details of the psychological methods to be used (something that can only be sensibly discussed in collaboration with the psychologists likely to be involved in the design of the regime and the running of the unit). The exact nature of the interactions between staff and inmates would again depend upon detailed choices about the psychological programme, though we would anticipate a high degree of staff involvement with prisoners.

130.   Although we do not wish at this stage to recommend in detail the kinds of psychologically-derived programme to be established for inmates in such a unit, we should place it on record that we have given some attention to the so-called 'token economy' systems which are already used in some institutions, especially for juveniles. (Token economy systems are a particular kind of social learning regime designed to modify behaviour by the use of tokens which function in broadly the same way as money in a national economic system: that is, target behaviours are made explicit, together with their token rewards, and tokens are then earned and used to buy reinforcers such as activities, consumables or privileges.) In our view, a token economy system is unlikely to be successful in meeting the presenting problems of adult disruptive prisoners, and we do not advocate its use in the specialist psychologically-based unit that we would like to see established.

131.   The second additional unit should in our view develop some of the ideas outlined in paragraphs 77 to 80 above. That is, it should draw its inspiration partly from the existing literature on the sociology of imprisonment; partly from developed practical experience of shared staff/prisoner discussion in institutions such as the Barlinnie Special Unit, Grendon Prison and the Wormwood Scrubs Annexe; and partly from the early lessons of the research programme which we have recommended in Section Three above. Drawing on these sources, it should develop a regime which regards the interaction between staff and prisoners as being a central issue in the genesis of the problem behaviour of some prisoners, and then, in effect, treats the question of social order within the prison as a key issue to be continually discussed by staff and inmates within the unit, in the hope that from the discussions it may prove possible for prisoners to return to normal dispersal locations with less friction than before. We anticipate that such a regime would have a low degree of structure, though there should be a requirement for prisoners to engage in collective discussion. We anticipate also that there would be a very high degree of staff involvement with prisoners, a high degree of prisoner participation in decisions about the way in which the unit operates, and a high degree of involvement by prisoners in finding ways of modifying their own problem behaviour.

132.   Although a regime of this type would obviously draw heavily on the Scottish experience at the Barlinnie Special Unit, we wish to emphasise that we

are not recommending a simple copy of that regime. In the first place, there are some features of the Barlinnie regime (for example, the very liberal visiting arrangements) which would in our view be inappropriate in the context of a special unit holding a number of maximum security prisoners. Secondly, the Barlinnie Special Unit drew its original inspiration from the notion of the 'therapeutic community', which is a rather different starting-point from that outlined in pargraphs 77 to 80. And thirdly, as indicated in the previous paragraph, the Barlinnie experience would only be one of several sources to draw upon in developing the details of the regime; careful consideration of the other sources may well lead to a number of modifications of the Barlinnie approach.

133. We *recommend* that the Prison Department should develop regime briefs for the Frankland and Milton Keynes sites based on the concepts outlined in paragraphs 129 to 132. While we are content with the action on special units which the Department has taken so far, we believe that an important opportunity will have been missed if the remaining units are not used to explore further regime possibilities, and we consider that the additional types of regime we have recommended have potential for dealing effectively with some control problem prisoners within an integrated but varied network of small units. We also *recommend* that every effort be made to build systematically upon the experience in and research results concerning all the special units as the system develops.

Consent

134. We would anticipate that some of the prisoners who persistently present serious control problems in the long-term prisons will welcome the opportunity offered by the special units of finding a way out of the vicious circle of misbehaviour — punishment — misbehaviour in which they seem to be trapped. Other prisoners, however, may not wish to be transferred to a special unit or to stay there once they have been transferred. They may, for example, want to move nearer their family or they may not like the regime the unit operates or they may simply not wish to co-operate with the prison authorities in any way whatsoever.

135. The legal position is that where a prisoner is located is the decision of, or on behalf of, the Secretary of State and does not require a prisoner's consent. The Department recognises, however, that certain therapeutic and training activities are not likely to be beneficial — and, indeed, may not be practicable — unless the prisoner participates willingly. Accordingly it has been the practice not to allocate a prisoner to Grendon to participate in the group-based regime there except with his agreement. With regard to medical treatment, within the prison system no medical treatment is given to a prisoner without his consent except in circumstances where treatment without consent

may be given as a matter of law and medical ethics in the outside community (summarised in section 62 of the Mental Health Act 1983)[22].

136. It is against this background that we have considered the question of whether transfer to a special unit should take place only with the inmate's agreement. We are sure that there is much to be said for trying to enlist the prisoner's interest in being transferred to a special unit and we think that for certain kinds of regime (for example, a social learning regime) this might be particularly desirable. But, we recognise that the units will not be able to play their part in the management of the most difficult and disruptive prisoners if such prisoners are given a choice as to whether they transfer to a special unit or not.

137. We have also considered whether inmates who have been in a special unit for a resonable length of time should be given the opportunity to leave if they wish. Our general conclusion is that this would not be practicable. We recognise, however, that distinct issues arise in relation to a unit such as C Wing, Parkhurst which has significant medical support and is explicitly therapeutic in intent.

138. At our suggestion, therefore, the Department discussed with the C Wing, Parkhurst management whether an inmate should be given the option to transfer elsewhere is he wished after his first 10 weeks in the unit. The Department concluded, after discussion, that a rule of this kind was undesirable and was required neither by law nor medical ethics.

139. The Department has made it clear that in C Wing, as elsewhere in the prison system, medical or other specialist therapies (such as group or individual therapy or counselling sessions conducted by a psychiatrist or psychologist) will not be undertaken unless the prisoners concerned consent to participate. Given that inmates will not be forced to accept medical treatment or to take part in group or individual sessions with specialists without their consent, the remaining elements of the unit's regime — work, education, exercise, association with other prisoners, contact with prison officers — are essentially no different from those to be found elsewhere in the prison system in units which have no specialist medical input.

140. The Department takes the view that there might be circumstances in which it would make sense to continue holding a prisoner in C Wing, Parkhurst notwithstanding his expressed wish to leave and/or his refusal to participate in regime activities. Many of the unit's inmates will have spent long periods on punishment, in segregation or in restricted association in prison hospitals prior to their transfer to C Wing. Such prisoners may have developed deeply entrenched patterns of solitary, unco-operative or violent behaviour or

---

22. Section 62 of the Mental Health Act 1983 recognises the common law position that a patient may be treated without his consent if the treatment is immediately necessary (i) to save his life, (ii) to prevent his condition seriously deteriorating, (iii) to alleviate serious suffering or (iv) to prevent the patient from behaving violently or being a danger to himself or others. In the case of (ii) the treatment should not be irreversible; in the case of (iii) and (iv) it should not be irreversible or hazardous.

attitudes towards staff and authority which, even in the most positive environment, may change only very slowly — if they change at all. In these circumstances it may not be realistic to expect to see a marked change in behaviour over a short period.

141. It may be, however, that after 10 weeks in the unit there are signs that a prisoner may be beginning — perhaps for the first time in years — to form positive relationships with staff or other prisoners, or to develop a more positive self-image, or to come to terms with the fact that he needs help with a behavioural or mental problem; or it may be that his behaviour seems to be marginally better in the unit than it was in any of his previous locations, or that staff are beginning to find ways of dealing with him that are less stressful for all concerned. At the very lowest level the judgement might be that, although the prisoner will continue to be disturbed and unco-operative for the forseeable future, the unit's regime nevertheless represents the best environ- ment available for him in the prison system. In any of these circumstances the conclusion might be that it would be in the interests of the prisoner and/or of the prison system to continue holding him in the unit.

142. What the Department has concluded in effect is that there might be good reasons for keeping a prisoner in the unit without his consent or co-operation and that, while in general they would take a wish to move at the 10 week review stage as an indication that an alternative location should be considered, a transfer would not be automatic in these circumstances. They would expect SUSC (whose members include the Medical Officer attached to the Parkhurst Unit and a representative of the Director of the Prison Medical Service) to look at each case on its merits and to take a decision about the best location for each prisoner in the light of all the available information. If after full consideration and discussion of alternative locations the medical members of SUSC considered that there were objections on the grounds of medical ethics to a prisoner continuing in the unit, then he would be transferred.

143. To summarise, the Department's conclusions are as follows. Prisoners will be transferred to the special units on the basis of a decision by the Special Units Selection Committee; after 10 weeks (and at regular intervals thereafter) SUSC will review each inmate's location and decide whether it is in his best interests or the best interests of the prison system for him to remain in the unit or be transferred elsewhere. At no stage in this process will the prisoner be asked for his formal consent to remaining in a unit, although his wishes will be one of the factors that SUSC will take into account in reaching its decisions. No prisoner will receive medical treatment or be required to take part in therapy sessions conducted by a psychiatrist or psychologist without his consent (except in the circumstances permitted under section 62 of the Mental Health Act 1983).

144. The position summarised in the previous paragraph has the full agreement of us all. We should record, however, that one of our former members, Professor Roy King, was unable to accept this position in relation to

C Wing, Parkhurst. In the case of the Parkhurst Unit Professor King took the view that there is a clear therapeutic intent behind the establishment of the unit, such that the nature of the regime amounts to a 'therapeutic' regime as that has been commonly construed in the literature. He, therefore, considered that it would be more appropriate for prisoners not to remain in the Parkhurst Unit without their consent after the first 10 week review.

Summary

145.   If our plans are realised a special unit system on the following lines will have been created by 1992:

Parkhurst

A special unit in a dispersal prison context operating a regime that is characterised by:

(i)   specialist assistant of a **psychiatric** nature in the form of:

- the availability of psychiatric treatment for inmates;

- advice and support to management and staff in their dealings with particular inmates;

- a general underpinning of the regime by psychiatric knowledge and skills;

and specialist assistance of a **psychological** nature in the form of:

- the availability of counselling and 'social learning' therapy programmes to inmates;

- advice and support to management and staff in their dealings with particular inmates;

(ii)   a moderate degree of structure;

(iii)   a high degree of staff involvement with prisoners;

(iv)   the promotion of some opportunities for prisoners to become involved in finding ways of modifying their own problem behaviour;

(v)   no inmate participation in the running of the unit.

Lincoln

A special unit in a local prison context operating a regime that is characterised by:

(i)   specialist assistance of a **psychological** nature in the form of advice and support to management and staff in their dealings with particular inmates;

(ii)   a higher degree of structure than the Parkhurst Unit;

(iii) a high degree of staff involvement with prisoners;

(iv) opportunities for prisoners to become involved in finding ways of modifying their own problem behaviour (in so far as these opportunities emerge in the natural interaction between prisoners and staff);

(v) no inmate participation in the running of the unit.

Hull

A special unit in the context of a local prison with recent dispersal experience operating a regime characterised by:

(i) specialist assistance of a **psychological** nature in the form of:

- the availability of counselling and 'social learning' therapy programmes to individual inmates;

- advice and support to management and staff in their dealings with individual prisoners;

(ii) a degree of structure broadly similar to that found in a normal dispersal prison wing;

(iii) a high degree of staff involvement with prisoners;

(iv) the promotion of some opportunities for prisoners to become involved in finding ways of modifying their own problem behaviour;

(v) no inmate participation in the running of the unit.

Frankland and Milton Keynes

A special unit in a dispersal prison context and a special unit in the context of a new local prison (which we hope will be built to 'new generation' designs) each operating one of the following regimes:

Option 1

A regime characterised by:

(i) specialist assistance of a **psychological** nature in the form of:

- a regime informed by and organised according to psychological principles;

- the availability of psychological programmes, counselling and group therapy to inmates;

- advice and support to management and staff in their dealings with individual inmates.

(ii) The appropriate degree of structure and the nature of the interactions between staff and inmates will be determined in the light of the choices made about the details of the psychological methods to be used; we would however anticipate a high degree of staff involvement with prisoners.

Option 2

A regime characterised by:

(i)   specialist assistance of a **sociological and social psychological** nature in the form of a regime drawing its inspiration partly from the existing literature on the sociology of imprisonment; partly from the empirical experience of Grendon, the Barlinnie Special Unit and the Wormwood Scrubs Annexe; and partly from the early lessons of the research programme outlined in Annex D;

(ii)   a low degree of structure;

(iii)   a very high degree of staff involvement with prisoners;

(iv)   a high degree of prisoner participation in decisions about the way in which the unit operates;

(v)   the involvement of prisoners to a high degree in finding ways of modifying their own problem behaviour.

Annex A
Membership of the Research and Advisory Group on the Long-Term Prison System

Chairman:

Mr S G Norris
(Mr A J Langdon)

Director of Operational Policy,
Prison Department.

Professor A E Bottoms

Director of the Institute of Criminology,
University of Cambridge.

Mr A J Butler
(Miss P C Drew)

Assistant Secretary, P3 Division, Prison
Department.

Miss M A Clayton
(Mr T C Platt)

Director of Regimes and Services, Prison
Department.

Mr I Dunbar

Regional Director (South West), Prison
Department.

Professor J Gunn

Institute of Psychiatry, University of London.

Dr J Kilgour

Director of the Prison Medical Service.

Mr M Williams

Principal Psychologist, Adult Offender
Psychology Unit, Prison Department.

Mr G R Walmsley

Principal Research Officer, Home Office
Research and Planning Unit.

Secretary:

Ms E B Moody

Principal, P3 Division, Prison Department.

Assistant Secretary:

Mr B Patterson
(Miss P M Teare)

HEO, P3 Division, Prison Department.

Names in brackets indicate former members who have since moved to other posts. In addition **Professor R D King** of the University College of North Wales and **Mrs M Tuck** (Head of the Home Office Research and Planning Unit) were members of the Group from November 1984 to November 1986 and November 1984 to January 1986 respectively.

Annex B
The Control Review
Committee's Recommendations

The Prison Department has compiled the following summary of the progress made in implementing the CRC's recommendations (at end January 1987):

CRC Recommendation	Accepted or Rejected	Position as at January 1987
LONG-TERM POSSIBILITIES FOR THE DISPERSAL SYSTEM		
(i) there should be an urgent examination of the possibilities of the US 'new generation' prison designs.	Accepted	Following the publication of the CRC Report, the Home Secretary established a Working Party to consider recent developments in US prison design. Its report – *New Directions in Prison Design** – was published in December 1985. Two new local prisons in the building programme (Milton Keynes and Doncaster) are currently being designed on 'new generation' lines; subject to satisfactory financial appraisal of these projects, other new prisons in the building programme are likely to adopt similar design principles.
		When the new dispersal prison at Full Sutton is open and there has been further experience of the special units in operation, the Department will consider the implications of the 'new generation' designs for long-term maximum security prisons.

* HMSO, 1985

CRC Recommendation	Accepted or Rejected	Position as at January 1987
PLANNING LONG-TERM PRISONERS' SENTENCES (ii) prisoners serving long sentences should be given the opportunity of spending a substantial part of their sentence in prisons that offer a relatively open regime.	Accepted	Long-term prisoners already have this opportunity in the dispersal system.
(iii) there should be a clear connection between a prisoner's behaviour and the course of his prison career.	Accepted	This recommendation was a statement of principle. For specific action see recommendations (iv) to (vii) below.
(iv)(a) prisoners serving more than 5 years should be thoroughly assessed during their first year and given individual sentence plans.	Decision deferred pending consideration of how this might be achieved in practice	A Prison Department working group is currently considering how this recommendation might be implemented (see also recommendation (vii) below).
(iv)(b) sentence planning units should be established in selected locals to carry out this work.	Rejected	Since the CRC reported, the prison population has risen and the local prisons in particular are now under more pressure. In these circumstances the Prison Department has concluded that it is not practicable to require local prisons to take on the additional burden of holding and assessing all long-term prisoners for 12 months. The working group referred to at recommendation (iv)(a) is considering the implications of this.

CRC Recommendation	Accepted or Rejected	Position as at January 1987
(v) and (vi) lifers should spend their first year in a sentence planning unit in a local then move to complete their 3 year assessment at a lifer main centre. Two small sentence planning units should be established in dispersals for Category As.	Rejected	These recommendations were dependent on the establishment of sentence planning units in local prisons. The Department has decided that that would not be practicable (see recommendation (iv)(b) above).
(vii) prisoners serving over 5 years should be centrally allocated.	Decision deferred pending consideration of how this might be implemented.	A Prison Department working group is currently considering how this recommendation might be implemented (see also recommendation (iv)(a) above).
DEALING WITH PRISONERS WHO PRESENT SERIOUS CONTROL PROBLEMS (viii) CI 10/74 should be made available to all Category B training prisons.	Rejected	The Department has concluded that such an extension is not required at present, although the situation will be kept under review in the light of developments concerning central allocation of long-termers.
(ix) those who persistently disrupt normal long-term prison life must be held elsewhere.	Accepted	This recommendation was a statement of principle. For specific action see recommendations (xiii) and (xiv) below.

CRC Recommendation	Accepted or Rejected	Position as at January 1987
(x) prisoners who present serious control problems in dispersals should be returned to sentence planning units for reallocation.	Rejected	This recommendation falls in the light of the Department's decision not to establish sentence planning units in local prisons.
(xi) special facilities should be provided for mentally disturbed prisoners whose instability or aggression presents a control problem.	Accepted	See recommendations (xii) and (xiii) below.
(xii) the prospect of developing the therapeutic regime at Grendon has much to offer.	Accepted	The first report of the Advisory Committee on the Therapeutic Regime at Grendon was published in July 1985. Its central recommendations have been accepted and are now being taken forward. No change is planned to the therapeutic regime, but an induction unit has been created and part of the hospital will be converted for use as an acute psychiatric unit. When a prisoner is referred for a place in a special unit the Special Units Selection Committee also considers whether the prisoner should be considered for a transfer to Grendon.
(xiii) a therapeutic facility should be established at C Wing, Parkhurst and the possibility of a subsequent similar unit considered in the light of experience.	Accepted	A special unit for prisoners with a history of both troublesome prison behaviour and of psychiatric abnormality was opened at C Wing, Parkhurst in December 1985. Its operation is being monitored and evaluated with the help of outside researchers but it is too early yet to decide whether a second similar unit should be established.

CRC Recommendation	Accepted or Rejected	Position as at January 1987
(xiv) a number of small units operating a variety of regimes should be established for prisoners who present control problems.	Accepted	The first special unit opened at C Wing, Parkhurst in December 1985 (see recommendation (xiii) above). A second unit is planned to open at Lincoln Prison in May 1987 and a third at Hull Prison in March 1988. Further units are planned for subsequent years.
(xv) the operation of all units should be centrally directed and their effectiveness monitored with outside participation.	Accepted	The special unit regimes are being designed with assistance from the Research and Advisory Group on the Long-Term Prison System (which includes outside academics) and outside researchers will be involved in the monitoring and evaluation of the units. Inmates are allocated into and out of the units by a central committee established at Prison Department Headquarters (the Special Units Selection Committee).
(xvi) more Rule 43 OP units are needed to ease control problems.	Accepted in principle.	A new Vulnerable Prisoner Unit was opened at Albany in 1985. The Department is currently considering whether any further units are required.
(xvii) the categorisation system should be reviewed in the light of developments in other penal systems.	Accepted	A survey of categorisation procedures in the USA has been undertaken on the Department's behalf by an outside researcher. The Department is currently reviewing its own categorisation procedures.

CRC Recommendation	Accepted or Rejected	Position as at January 1987
(xviii) and (xix) individual prisons should be set clearly defined objectives within the framework of a national policy on long-term imprisonment. Regime activities should be planned centrally.	Accepted in principle.	Under the new procedures introduced by Circular Instruction 55/84 Governors now agree objectives annually with Regional Directors. Those staff responsible for the central allocation of life sentence prisoners will identify the activities they require in prisons taking lifers and specify these requirements to Regional Directors so that they can be taken into account in the annual contracts agreed under CI 55/84. In the longer term it is envisaged that a similar role would be played by those responsible for the central allocation of determinate sentence long-termers.
(xx) regime activities should be provided by way of individual prisoner programmes.	Decision deferred pending consideration of how this recommendation might be implemented.	Work on this front is being taken forward in the context of continuing development of the procedures under CI 55/84. In addition, Mr Dunbar, now Regional Director (SW), and a member of RAG, was seconded to the Prisons Inspectorate for 6 months to undertake a comparative study of the delivery of regime activities in various overseas countries. His Report, *A Sense of Direction**, was published in October 1985.

*   Home Office, 1985

CRC Recommendation	Accepted or Rejected	Position as at January 1987
(xxi) incentives should be developed in Category C and D establishments to make security down-grading and progression psychologically credible.	Accepted	Additional privileges have been introduced in Category D establishments: since April 1986 there has been no limit on the number of letters prisoners may send and receive; there are earlier and more frequent opportunities for home leave; and payphones are being installed for the use of prisoners. The Department accepts the logic of extending these privileges to Category C prisons, but it intends to evaluate the experience of these changes at open establishments before proceeding further. This evaluation will take place in the context of a wider consideration of Category C and D regimes by a Prison Department working group which will begin early in 1987.
(xxii) there should be a statement of the basic objectives of imprisonment.	Accepted	The objectives of the sentence of imprisonment are set out in Chapters 3 and 9 of *The Sentence of the Court**. The Prisons Board has defined the tasks of the Prison Service and the functions of Prison Service establishments in CI 55/84 (published as Appendix 7 to the *Report on the work of the Prison Department 1984/85)#*. This CI sets out the arrangements for defining operational objectives for fulfilling these tasks and functions. The Department has given priority to developing systems for setting and measuring the achievement of regime targets consistent with the tasks and functions of the Service. The case for a further statement of the objectives of imprisonment will be assessed when these systems have been developed.

*   HMSO, 1986
#   Cmnd 9699, HMSO, 1985

CRC Recommendation	Accepted or Rejected	Position as at January 1987
THE SIZE OF THE DISPERSAL SYSTEM (xxiii) Wormwood Scrubs and one other dispersal should be down-graded in security.	Accepted	Hull Prison was taken out of the dispersal system in February 1986 and converted to a local prison (with the exception of A Wing which will be converted for use as a special unit to open in March 1988). The number of dispersal prisons will be kept under review by the Department as the special units develop with particular reference to the possibility that D Hall at Wormwood Scrubs might cease to have a dispersal role.
STAFF DIMENSION (xxiv) there should be a movement towards more structured arrangements for the career development of prison officers.	Accepted in principle	If the proposals to devolve certain personnel functions to Regions bear fruit the matter will be reviewed in the light of the staffing levels then obtaining.
(xxv) considerable emphasis should be put on staff training in long-term prisons.	Accepted	Funds have been made available for additional training for special unit staff. (See also recommendation (xxvii) below.)
(xxvi) an effective communications struc-ture between manage-ment and staff is very important in long-term prisons.	Accepted	Improvements in communications will be one of the primary aims of the revision of management struc-tures in all Prison Service establish-ments to be conducted as part of the implementation of the 'Fresh Start' proposals. These proposals were published in July and November 1986. Their implementation is targeted for 1 April 1987, dependent on the progress of discussion with the Prison Service trade unions.

CRC Recommendation	Accepted or Rejected	Position as at January 1987
(xxvii) higher security prisons should have adequate cover of staff trained in MUFTI and personal restraint techniques.	Accepted	MUFTI resources are available or can be summoned at all dispersal prisons. Control and restraint training has been given very high priority and special emphasis has been placed on the needs of dispersal prisons.
(xxviii) there should be recognition of the stress on dispersal staff.	Accepted	Four of the seven dispersal prisons attract an inconvenience of locality allowance which permits a move at public expense after 7 years. All requests for a move on grounds of stress which are supported by medical evidence are considered sympathetically and a Departmental working party on occupational health is currently looking at the question of stress in the course of its work.
(xxix) greater attention should be paid to the minor details of prison design.	Accepted	The current review of the prison briefing guides may provide an opportunity to take this recommendation forward in specific contexts.
RESEARCH (xxx) a research programme into the control aspect of running the prison system should be established with the help of outside experts.	Accepted	The Research and Advisory Group on the Long-Term Prison System (whose members include outside academics) was set up in November 1984. On the basis of this Group's advice research addressing control issues has been included in the Home Office's funded research programme.

Annex C
Identifying 'Difficult' Prisoners in Dispersal Prisons

Mark Williams and David Longley, Adult Offender Psychology Unit

Introduction

Implicit in the search for an accurate and objective procedure to identify 'difficult' prisoners is a test of the validity of the concept of the 'difficult prisoner' itself. Using identification of putative difficult prisoners as the starting point, evidence bearing on this issue may be collected under several different but related headings:

(i)   the extent to which objective indices of 'difficulty' correlate, and support the notion of relatively stable individual differences in degree of 'difficulty';

(ii)   the characteristics of the judgements of prison staff as to who the 'difficult' prisoners are (for example, are those judgements consistent over time? Is there inter-judge reliability?);

(iii)   the characteristics of those prisoners identified as 'difficult', compared with those in the dispersal system not so identified;

(iv)   differences within the groups of prisoners identified as 'difficult', related to possible differences in approach to their management; and

(v)   the effects of acting on the results of these enquiries, along the lines recommended in the CRC report.

What follows is a brief description of the progress that has been made so far in some of the various studies directed along these lines.

Agreement between different measures of 'difficulty'

2.   From work already done for the CRC to discover the characteristics most directly related to 'difficulty', it was decided to follow a strategy concentrating on inter-prison movement where that movement was unambiguously related to bad behaviour. This was done by taking all those who were permanently transferred from a dispersal prison, during the period 1 January 1983 to 30 June 1984, following either:

(i)   at least 30 days segregation under Rule 43(GOAD), or

(ii)   temporary transfer for segregation under CI 10/74.

This produced 65 names, of which 10 occurred in both lists. Using the existing data-base for the current dispersal system, it was possible to compare them with a randomly-selected group of similar size, who were contemporaries of the problem group.

3. The most salient results of the comparison are shown in Table 1.

Table 1   Comparing transferred prisoners with other dispersal prisoners

	TRANSFERRED PRISONERS	COMPARISON GROUP
% Category A	49	16.1
% Life sentence	46	33
% 20+ Governors' Reports	83	18.3
% Violence to staff	61.5	13.4
% Violence to prisoners	44.5	15.9
% R43 (GOAD) this sentence	89.2	14.7

What these results suggest is that although there was no absolute distinction between the most difficult prisoners and the rest, there were nevertheless reasonable grounds for supposing that a significant minority of notably difficult prisoners existed, and that they could be identified (though not without some arbitrary decisions about criteria) using conventional measures. A more formal development of this line of enquiry was initiated in 1985.

Prisoners identified as 'difficult' in 1985

4. In January 1985 the names of possible candidates for the Special Units recommended by the CRC were sought from the major potential sources of referral, including:

(i)   the current Governors of the eight dispersal prisons;

(ii)   the section in HQ responsible for the allocation and management of prisoners having security Category A status (the 'Cat As'); and

(iii)   the section in HQ responsible for the allocation and management of life sentence prisoners (which excludes Category A lifers).

In addition, the Adult Offender Psychology Unit (AOPU) computer-file of movement and segregation within the dispersal system was used to provide the names of those who met the criteria set out earlier.

5. There are distinct limits to the degree to which different sources can agree as to which prisoners give rise to problems of control. The Category A and Life Sentence Sections in HQ provide lists that are mutually exclusive (being of different security categories). There are also apparent differences of definition of 'difficult' as between personnel in HQ and those in the actual prisons. And finally the numbers were very different, as is apparent from the detailed results of the trawl presented in Table 2. (Regional Offices and some non-dispersal prisons also contributed very disparate numbers.)

Table 2   **Numbers of potential special unit candidates nominated from different sources**

SOURCE OF NOMINATION:	NUMBER:
1. Governors of dispersal prisons	
a. HMP ALBANY	21
b. HMP FRANKLAND	18
c. HMP GARTREE	8
d. HMP HULL	3
e. HMP LONG LARTIN	5
f. HMP PARKHURST	1
g. HMP WAKEFIELD	38
h. HMP WORMWOOD SCRUBS	14
2. Regional Offices:	
a. NORTH REGIONAL OFFICE	0
b. MIDLAND REGIONAL OFFICE	9
c. SOUTH EAST REGIONAL OFFICE	0
d. SOUTH WEST REGIONAL OFFICE	25
3. HQ P2 Division (Life Sentence Section)	41
4. HQ P3 Division (Category A Section)	32
5. Governors of Category B training prisons	
a. HMP DARTMOOR	0
b. HMP MAIDSTONE	10
6. The Adult Offender Psychology Unit	62
Total:	287

In all, of the 287 names put forward, 226 were unique.

6.   Agreement between the different sources was organized according to category of prisoner. For the 73 Category A prisoners, the majority (41) were nominated by one source only; the details are set out in Table 3.

Table 3   **The identification of the same Category A prisoners as special unit candidates by different referral sources**

SOURCE(S)	NUMBER
Governors only	22
Category A Section only	10
AOP Unit only	8
Region	1
Governors, Category A Section	9
Governors, AOP Unit	7
Governors, Region	3
Category A Section, AOP Unit	4
Governors, Category A Section, AOP Unit	7
Governors, Category A Section, Region	1
Governors, Cat A Section, AOP Unit, Region	1

For the Category Bs, the result may be summed up rather more succinctly: of the 151 names, only 12 were mentioned twice, and only one was mentioned three times. Lifer Section also recommended two Category C prisoners, of which all other sources could only be ignorant. It is apparent therefore, that although there is modest agreement as to who constitute the problem-cases among the Category A prisoners, there is very little as to the remainder.

7.   Initially, analysis of this group of 'difficult' prisoners was restricted to those nominated by the dispersal prison Governors, the HQ sections and the AOP Unit. This was because the lists produced by these four sources were exhaustive, whereas the Regional Offices and non-dispersal Category B prisons were only partially represented. To compare with the 170 'difficult' prisoners a random sample of 175 prisoners was taken from the dispersal system database, after all those nominated as 'difficult' had been excluded. Seventeen characteristics were considered, and the basic comparisons are presented in Table 4.

Table 4   **Comparing 'difficult' prisoners with other dispersal prisoners**

CHARACTERISTIC:	% OF 'DIFFICULT' (N = 170):	% OF OTHERS (N = 175):
1. Date of birth pre-1952	45.9	45.1
2. Serving a life sentence	51.8	27.4
3. Sentence date post-1979	56.5	84.6
4. Offence of murder, attempted murder	50.6	30.9
5. Offence of robbery	24.1	32.0
6. Previous offence of robbery	25.9	25.7
7. Previous offence of violence	60.0	49.1
8. Previous convictions greater than 3	77.6	71.4
9. Previous custodial sentences > 1	68.2	58.3
10. Governor's reports greater than 19	51.8	7.4
11. Staff assaults greater than 1	34.1	4.6
12. Inmate assaults greater than 1	21.8	5.1
13. Previous prisons this sentence > 2	70.6	20.6
14. Category A	40.0	8.6
15. Rule 43 (GOAD) > 2 occasions	16.5	1.7
16. Any incident of self-injury	25.3	13.7
17. Previous psychiatric history	21.8	9.1

The major distinctions are obvious: the prisoners identified as 'difficult' are more violent (items 4, 7, 11, 12), have been deemed more dangerous (item 14), have been involved in more trouble inside prison (items 10, 11, 13) and are more disturbed (items 16 and 17).

8.   The four sources were contrasted with respect to these same characteristics, and for the central qualities were very similar. Of course, by definition some characteristics were strongly represented by one particular source: Category A by the Category A Section, the life sentence by the Lifer Section, and a history of segregation under Rule 43(GOAD) by the AOP Unit.

The second trawl: July 1985

9.   The dispersal prison governors were asked to provide a second list of potential special unit candidates in July 1985, six months after the first request. The numbers put forward from the individual prisons are given in Table 5.

Table 5   **Numbers nominated on Trawl 1 and Trawl 2**

DISPERSAL PRISON:	TRAWL 1	TRAWL 2
a. HMP ALBANY	21	16
b. HMP FRANKLAND	18	6
c. HMP GARTREE	8	9
d. HMP HULL	3	3
e. HMP LONG LARTIN	5	2
f. HMP PARKHURST	1	24
g. HMP WAKEFIELD	38	20
h. HMP WORMWOOD SCRUBS	14	21
Totals:	108	101

10.   This second trawl revealed some of the practical or organizational problems of such an exercise that exist in addition to the conceptual, even within a single referral-source. Only 54 of the 106 Governor-nominees were still in their original prison (of the 108 nominations, two had been nominated twice, leaving a sample of 106 actual prisoners); 12 had either been released or their release was imminent; there was ambiguity as to whether or not those accepted for transfer to a Special Hospital should still be included; and some were no longer in the dispersal system. Details of the status of the initial Governor-nominees are presented in Table 6.

Table 6   **Inmates nominated by Governors in January 1985:**
their status in the July 1985 Trawl

RENOMINATED:	
In original dispersal prison	32
Nominated by a different dispersal prison	10
Nominated by original dispersal after transfer	8
NOT RENOMINATED:	
In original dispersal prison	22
Special Hospital transfers	4
Transferred outside dispersal system	15
Transferred within dispersal system	15
TOTAL:	106

11.   Similar details for the new additions are given in Table 7. The variability in the process may be gauged from the fact that from the original list of 106 Governor-nominees, the second trawl omitted 56 old names and added 48 new ones. And these changes in status occurred for a large proportion of inmates who were in the same dispersal prison throughout the sampling period (22 of the 56 who were dropped, and 25 of the 48 who were added).

Table 7   **Status of inmates nominated by Governors in July 1985 who had not been nominated in January 1985**

Located in same dispersal prison in January and July	25
Located in a different dispersal prison	15
Located in a non-dispersal prison in January	8
TOTAL:	48

12.   In addition to the dispersal system governors, other sources (where appropriate) were also trawled a second time. To the totals from the first trawl presented in Table 2 (287 nominees, representing 226 different individuals) the second trawl added a further 138 names, creating a final total of 270 individual prisoners. Details are set out in Table 8.

Table 8   **Sample details of two trawls**

Trawl:	1	2
Total of nominations:	287	138
Total of individuals:	226	127

270 UNIQUE NAMES OVERALL

13.   Whatever the uncertainty about the process of nomination, objective evidence confirms that the nominees of every status differ from their peers in the dispersal system. The total set of 'difficult' prisoners identified by the two separate trawls scored significantly higher on an objective schedule to determine a prisoner's custody rating (designed by the National Institute of Corrections to categorize the prisoners presenting control problems within American prisons; see the 1982 reference) than did a non-problem sample matched for date and length of sentence who were also held in the dispersal system. The mean scores for the groups are presented in Table 9.

Table 9 N.I.C. Custody (Reclassification) Scores for 'difficult' and non-problem samples

Columns:
- Nominations
- 'DIFFICULT' SAMPLE NOMINATED BY ALL SOURCES: No, NIC SCORE Mean, S.E
- 'DIFFICULT' SAMPLE NOMINATED BY GOVERNORS ONLY: No, NIC SCORE Mean, S.E
- NON-PROBLEM SAMPLE: No, NIC SCORE Mean, S.E

Rows:
Either occasion: 203, 12.5, 0.60 | 135, 13.5, 0.73 | 208, 5.4, 0.46
Both occasions: 63, 14.8, 1.07 | 41, 14.2, 1.40 | —, —, —
Only first time: 93, 11.2, 0.86 | 47, 13.1, 1.25 | —, —, —
Only second time: 47, 11.9, 1.22 | 47, 13.2, 1.18 | —, —, —Table 9   **N.I.C. Custody (Reclassification) Scores for 'difficult' and non-problem samples**

Nominations:	'DIFFICULT' SAMPLE NOMINATED BY ALL SOURCES			'DIFFICULT' SAMPLE NOMINATED BY GOVERNORS ONLY			NON-PROBLEM SAMPLE		
	No:	NIC SCORE: Mean	S.E	No:	NIC SCORE: Mean	S.E	No:	NIC SCORE: Mean	S.E
Either occasion	203	12.5	0.60	135	13.5	0.73	208	5.4	0.46
Both occasions	63	14.8	1.07	41	14.2	1.40	—	—	—
Only first time	93	11.2	0.86	47	13.1	1.25	—	—	—
Only second time	47	11.9	1.22	47	13.2	1.18	—	—	—

(numbers completed at the time of going to press)

14.   Considering the nature of the comparison group, the NIC scores discriminate very well between the various sets of prisoners, all of whom were currently in the dispersal system. This is particularly so for the basic contrast between the 'difficult' prisoners (defined as anyone identified in either trawl) and the matched sample of dispersal prisoners who were not identified as presenting a control problem. The actual distribution of NIC scores for these two groups are presented in Figure 1 (and the numbers are quite large: 203 prisoners presenting control problems and 208 non-problem prisoners — although matched, some NIC scores are still unavailable so the numbers are not exactly equal).

Figure 1: **Distribution of Total Scores on N.I.C. Custody Rating Scale**

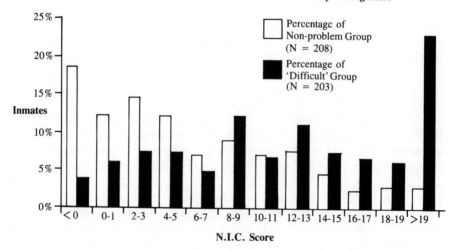

Conclusion

15.   This paper has been very much a description of work in progress, and the work is continuing. There now exists a well-defined sample of 'difficult' prisoners and a matched group of long-term inmates of the dispersal system. The information about these groups, when complete, will provide the basis for a systematic analysis of the differences between and within them. Without this information, the results of the work so far are often difficult to interpret, but certain elements seem to be clear:

(i)   some prisoners are reliably identified as presenting problems in the dispersal prison system, and exhibit distinctive characteristics when compared to their peers;

(ii)   considerable difficulties remain in their identification, and in our understanding of the nature of those difficulties;

(iii)   nevertheless, there is considerable evidence that it will be possible to define some objective procedure for at least the initiation of the process of identifying and dealing with the members of this minority.

16.   However the prisoners presenting control problems are ultimately to be identified, it is possible to argue that a central element to any objective part of the procedure should be the number of different prisons in which the sentence has been served (taking account of length of sentence, of course). There is ample evidence that this index is a key 'symptom' of 'difficulty'. In Figure 2 the same comparison between the 'difficult' prisoners and their matched controls as in Figure 1 is presented, but this time based on number of prisons this sentence (obviously an inferior measure to disciplinary transfers, but even so, sufficient to demonstrate the contrast).

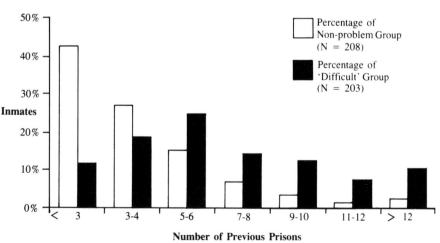

Figure 2: **Distribution of Previous Prisons**

Number of Previous Prisons

17. Apart from these empirical considerations, however, there are other arguments in favour of the importance of disciplinary transfers in identifying 'difficult' prisoners:

(i) disciplinary transfer can be routinely recorded and as a measure it is unambiguous;

(ii) as an index of 'difficulty', disciplinary transfer represents a central element of that 'difficulty' in that it reflects the interaction between the particular prisoner and the particular prison;

(iii) as a process, disciplinary transfer is the natural 'emergency' response to prisoners presenting control problems (arguably preferable to segregation);

(iv) as a record, the number of disciplinary transfers not only alerts us to the really difficult inmate; it also allows inspection that all the alternative locations have been tried (or what alternative locations remain before consideration for special treatment should be considered).

The collation and analysis of disciplinary transfer data is currently being pursued.

Reference

National Institute of Corrections, (1982). Prison Classification: A Model Systems Approach. Washington DC.

Acknowledgements

Special thanks are extended to all field Psychologists and Psychological Assistants who collected the bulk of the data summarized in this paper.

Annex D
Research Programme

On our advice the following projects have been included in the Home Office Research and Planning Unit's current research programme:

1. Title: **PRISON REGIMES AND CONTROL: A LITERATURE SURVEY**

Research body: Research and Planning Unit

Description: A review of the literature on control in prisons, with special reference to prison regimes and management, including consideration of prison design and the nature of the population of an establishment insofar as they appear to assist or militate against the maintenance of control.

Comment: This review is now complete and a report is being prepared for publication.

2. Title: **CONTROL PROBLEMS AND THE LONG-TERM PRISONER**

Research body: Institute of Criminology, University of Cambridge.

Description: A study of the nature of control problems among long-term prisoners and of their emergence, including examination of the circumstances in which prisoners are transferred from normal location.

Comment: It is anticipated that a grant will be offered to the Institute of Criminology to commence work on a two-year project. The project would concentrate on two dispersal prisons which appear to differ in the frequency with which control problems emerge.

3. Title: **SPECIAL SECURITY UNITS**

Research body: Research and Planning Unit.

Description: A short study of the special security units in the prison system (currently the Special Security Block at HMP Parkhurst and the Special Security Wing at HMP Leicester).

Comment: This study which is due to be undertaken early in 1987 concentrates on aspects of the special security units that

63

may provide useful pointers in connection with the establishment of the special units for inmates presenting control problems, including regimes, relationships within the unit, length of stay, effects on host prisons and means of coping with control problems.

4. Title: **SPECIAL UNITS AND THE LONG-TERM PRISONER**

Research body: Various

Description: Descriptive and evaluative studies of the special units, with external involvement in the evaluation.

Comment: Research is already under way in respect of the first special unit at C Wing, Parkhurst. The psychologist attached to the Unit is keeping a diary of events and collecting a range of other data which will together be the basis of the descriptive account. Evaluative work of various types is either current or planned:

a.   psychiatric testing of inmates, being conducted by the Institute of Psychiatry, University of London, which will include a record of any changes in inmates' mental state during their time in the unit;

b.   psychological testing of inmates, by the unit psychologist, which will include a record of attitudinal changes in inmates;

c.   an assessment by an independent academic researcher, based on observation and informed judgement, which will include comment on features of the unit, events occuring in the unit, inmates' training plans and careers in the unit and the personal officer scheme;

d.   consideration of the effect of the unit on its host prison and vice versa;

e.   follow-up work on the subsequent behaviour in the prison system of inmates after they have left the unit.

The Steering Group for this research is a small sub-group of the Research and Advisory Group on the Long-Term Prison System. A report or reports on the first two years of the C Wing, Parkhurst unit (ie. to the end of December 1987) will include all aspects covered by the descriptive and evaluative studies. It is intended that the second special

64

unit at Lincoln, which is due to open in May 1987, and the Hull Unit, due to open in March 1988, shall be the subject of research on similar lines.

In addition we have an interest in the following projects which are also included in the Research and Planning Unit's current programme:

5. Title: **PSYCHIATRIC PROFILE OF THE PRISON POPULATION**

Research body: Institute of Psychiatry, University of London.

Description: A study of the nature and extent of psychiatric disorder, and the need for psychiatric treatment, among the prison population of England and Wales, including a description of existing arrangements for the management, care and treatment of mentally disordered inmates, and the identification of any therapeutic needs which are not being met under existing arrangements.

Comment: It is anticipated that a grant will be offered to the Institute of Psychiatry to commence work on this major project in the first half of 1987. The research is expected to take three years to complete.

6. Title: **THERAPEUTIC REGIME AT HMP GRENDON**

Research body: Centre for Criminological Research, University of Oxford.

Description: A study of the therapeutic regime at HMP Grendon and its function within the prison system.

Comment: This two-year project, which commenced in October 1986, sets out to understand the social organisation of Grendon, how it functions, and how it succeeds in managing inmates who have created disciplinary problems in other establishments. It will examine the processes of decision making in the selection and rejection of inmates for Grendon and will explore how the Grendon regime is perceived by professionals within the prison service. It will also assess the consequences of the Grendon experience for the management of long-term prisoners who are subsequently transferred back to an ordinary training prison.

Annex E
Special Unit in C Wing at HMP Parkhurst

The special unit at C Wing, Parkhurst opened in December 1985. It accepts long-term prisoners in Categories A and B who have a history of or who present symptoms of mental abnormality *and* who are currently presenting, and have persistently presented at more than one establishment, one or more of the following problem behaviours:

(i)   violence towards staff and/or prisoners;

(ii)   offences against discipline resulting in repeated formal reports;

(iii)   damage to property within institutions;

(iv)   other behaviour that is dangerous or disruptive.

2.   The unit has the following aims:

(i)   to provide a national resource for certain types of disruptive and disturbed prisoners who are at present contained largely in the dispersal system;

(ii)   to achieve a constructive way of managing such prisoners within a discrete unit by individualising the management of inmates and by encouraging a high degree of staff involvement;

(iii)   to facilitate observation of inmate behaviour in order that early signals of impending crisis can be identified and preventive or remedial action taken;

(iv)   to encourage attitude changes and improvements in the mental state, behaviour and social skills of the inmates.

Management and staffing

3.   The unit is headed by a Governor IV who is directly responsible to the Governor of Parkhurst Prison. He works with a management team consisting of a Medical Officer, a Senior Psychologist and a Hospital Chief Officer. The prison officers working in the unit are a mixture of discipline and hospital officers who previously worked in Parkhurst Prison and who were selected from among a large number of applicants. Additional specialist support is

provided by a full-time teacher and by a Probation Officer, Chaplain, PE Instructor and a second teacher from the main prison. Staff in all disciplines work closely together as a team.

Regime

4.   The unit seeks to provide a relaxed and safe environment in which troublesome prisoners, who may have spent significant periods of time segregated from others, can be encouraged to associate more freely with staff and other inmates. The general policy is one of non-confrontation. Staff are encouraged to use their interpersonal skills to prevent potentially dangerous situations arising and to deal with antagonistic behaviour. Formal disciplinary procedures are employed as a last resort.

5.   Each inmate arriving in the unit is assigned to a Personal Officer (and a deputy Personal Officer working opposite shifts). It is the responsibility of the Personal Officer to develop a close knowledge of his inmate, to monitor and record his behaviour and progress, and to build up a relationship with him. The Personal Officer is the inmate's first point of contact within the unit and nothing should happen to the inmate (except in an emergency) without his Personal Officer's knowledge.

6.   The inmate's first ten weeks in the unit are treated as an assessment period. During this time the Personal Officer and the specialist staff will assess his needs, his interests, his strengths and his weaknesses. At the end of this period a meeting is held of all concerned (including, where possible, the inmate himself) to draw up an individual 'training plan'. This document sets out the inmate's activities and targets (educational, behavioural, social as appropriate) for the following 15 weeks. Progress is reviewed every 15 weeks thereafter and the training plan amended as necessary.

7.   Prisoners are encouraged to spend as much time as possible out of their cells mixing with staff and other inmates. A range of activities (including work, education and PE) is available in the unit and the unit has its own workshop, gym, small kitchen and television rooms. Prisoners are, however, able to decline to take part in any of the activities on offer (with the alternative of remaining locked in their cell).

Inmate population

8.   The unit's population has risen gradually during its first twelve months and at the time of writing (December 1986) stands at 18. The table below shows the current inmate population in terms of their age, security category, length of sentence, previous location and their problem behaviours over the three years prior to their admission to C Wing.

9.   In terms of their behaviour in prison over the three years prior to arriving in C Wing, 4 of the inmates have been frequent and persistent offenders, having 40 or more offences against discipline. Similarly, 7 prisoners have

reports for violence to other inmates and 9 have been violent towards prison staff. During the same period, 3 inmates have seriously mutilated themselves or attempted suicide. In addition to the information shown in the table, it should be noted that three inmates have killed while in custody and one has been found guilty of attempted murder while in custody (although not all these events occurred in the three years prior to their admission to the unit).

10.   It is clear from the table, however, that some inmates in the unit do not appear to have been particularly problematic in behavioural terms. The rationale of their acceptance concerned the referring prison's worries about their potential dangerousness. The referring prisons argued that they had followed a policy of non-confrontation in order to avoid provocation and that as a result much of the inmate's difficult behaviour was ignored and would not be indicated in terms of reports against discipline.

11.   In the first twelve months of the unit's operation two prisoners have had to be permanently removed from the unit on the grounds that their behaviour threatened the stability of the unit as a whole. Two other prisoners have been returned to normal location in dispersal prisons after demonstrating a sustained improvement in behaviour.

Inmates allocated to C Wing as of January 1987

INMATE	AGE	PREVIOUS LOCATION	SENTENCE LENGTH	SECURITY CATEGORY	PAST THREE YEARS: SELF-MUTILATION/ SUICIDE ATTEMPTS	PAST THREE YEARS: INCIDENTS CONSTITUTING 'CONTROL PROBLEMS'			NUMBER OF REPORTS
						VIOLENCE TO STAFF	VIOLENCE TO INMATES	DAMAGE TO PROPERTY	
A	48	Dispersal hospital	LIFE	A	—	—	1	1	11
B	31	Dispersal normal location	LIFE	A	—	3	—	2	36
C	31	Dispersal hospital	LIFE	B	2	—	—	—	7
D	27	Dispersal segregation	LIFE	A	—	1	4	1	19
E	31	Dispersal segregation	11 years	B	—	13	2	5	63
F	41	Dispersal segregation	LIFE	A	—	—	1	—	6
G	38	Dispersal hospital	LIFE	A	1	—	—	—	—
H	38	Local segregation	25 years	B	—	12	—	5	99
I	35	Dispersal hospital	LIFE	A	2	3	—	2	11
J	40	Dispersal normal location	LIFE	B	—	—	—	—	11

Inmates allocated to C Wing as of January 1987 *(continued)*

INMATE	AGE	PREVIOUS LOCATION	SENTENCE LENGTH	SECURITY CATEGORY	PAST THREE YEARS: SELF-MUTILATION/ SUICIDE ATTEMPTS	PAST THREE YEARS: INCIDENTS CONSTITUTING 'CONTROL PROBLEMS'			
						VIOLENCE TO STAFF	VIOLENCE TO INMATES	DAMAGE TO PROPERTY	NUMBER OF REPORTS
K	39	Dispersal normal location	LIFE	A	—	—	—	—	—
L	37	Dispersal normal location	LIFE	A	—	—	—	—	4
M	36	Dispersal segregation	LIFE	A	—	4	1	9	41
N	40	Dispersal hospital	LIFE	A	—	—	—	—	14
O	39	Dispersal segregation	14 years	A	—	3	3	—	14
P	34	Category B segregation	4 years	B	—	3	—	—	19
Q	35	Dispersal segregation	LIFE	A	—	9	1	2	40
R	42	Dispersal normal location	LIFE	A	—	—	—	—	4

Annex F

Please type or print in black ink

Referral of a Prisoner for possible transfer to a Special Unit

To: P3 Division
Prison Department Headquarters
Cleland House

---

1. Please supply the following information about the inmate:

Full name:

Number:

PDP number:

Current prison and date of reception:

Security category:

Date of birth:

Age:

Ethnic origin *(by reference to C1 25/84)*:

Current offence(s):

Effective sentence:

Sentencing court:

Date of sentence:

EDR: LDR: PED:

Next LRC *(for lifers only)*:

Number of days remission lost:

Present location in current establishment *(eg normal, hospital, segregation)*:

If on temporary transfer, give location and reason for transfer:

2. Please list below all previous establishments (including special hospitals) with dates this sentence:

Establishments	Dates

3. Please tick below the ground(s) on which this prisoner is considered suitable for transfer to a special unit:

(i)   violence towards staff ☐
(ii) violence towards inmates ☐
(iii) repeated offences against discipline ☐
(iv) damage to property ☐
(v)   hostage taking ☐
(vi) barricading ☐
(vii) self mutilation ☐
(viii) suicide attempts ☐
(ix) other *(please give brief details)* ☐

Please continue on a separate page if necessary

4. Please give in date order details of all adjudications in each of the last 3 years and the nature of the offence *(eg assault on staff, assault on inmates, damage to property, disobeying an order)*:

Date	Offence

Please continue on a separate page if necessary

73

5. Please record below in date order periods spent on Rule 43 GOAD, on transfer under CI 10/74 or under punishment (on punishment landing or segregation unit) in the last three years:

Rule 43 GOAD or C.I. 10/74 or punishment	Dates		Total number of days
	From	To	

Please continue on a separate page if necessary

6. Please attach specialist reports from each of the following:

   Wing management *(AG, PO or Hospital PO as appropriate)* **(Form A)**
   Medical Officer **(Form B)**
   Security Officer **(Form C)**
   Landing/Personal Officer **(Form D)**
   Psychologist *(where appropriate)* **(Form E)**
   Probation Officer *(where appropriate)* **(Form F)**
   Other(s) *(please specify)* **(Form G)**

---

7. Please attach the following:

   Page 2a of F1150
   Page 3 of F1150
   Page 4 of F1150
   Page 20 of F1150
   Page 24 of F1150
   List of previous convictions
   Any other relevant reports *(eg reports to court)*

---

8. Governor's assessment of the prisoner *(to be completed by the Governor or Deputy Governor)*:

Governor's signature

Date:

Please continue on a separate page if necessary

Form A

Wing Management Report

(to be completed by the AG, PO or Hospital PO as appropriate)

Please give a pen picture of the prisoner, covering all the following points:

  (i)   social/family circumstances *(including any visits received)*;

  (ii) criminal history;

  (iii) circumstances of offence;

  (iv) prison behaviour *(including details of his strengths and weaknesses; interests; relationships with staff; relationships with other inmates; any particularly disruptive behaviour; efforts made in your establishment to control the prisoner's behaviour and the results)*:

Name: Signature:

Position: Date:

Please continue on a separate page if necessary

Medical/Psychiatric Report

(to be completed by the Medical Officer, visiting psychiatrist etc as appropriate)

1.   Please give a brief outline of the prisoner's psychiatric and medical history and the details of any treatment:

2.   Please give an assessment of the prisoner's current mental state and details of any current treatment:

Please continue on a separate page if necessary

Medical/Psychiatric Report *(continued)*

3.   Please state any medical restrictions on transfers:

4.   Please state if you consider that a transfer to C Wing, Parkhurst would be appropriate and explain why:

Name: Signature:

Position: Date:

Please continue on a separate page if necessary

78

Security Officer's Report

(to be completed by Security PO or SO)

1. Please give a brief account of any escape history and an assessment of escape potential:

2. Please state any special information which may be relevant to this referral *(eg inmates with whom the prisoner should not associate)*:

3. Any other comments:

Name: Signature:

Position: Date:

Please continue on a separate page if necessary

Landing/Personal Officer's Report

Please give a detailed pen picture of the prisoner *(including a description of his behaviour; his strengths and his weaknesses; his interests; and his relationships with staff and other inmates)*:

Name: Signature:

Position: Date:

Please continue on a separate page if necessary

Psychologist's Report

1. Please give brief details of any treatment/training programmes undertaken with this prisoner and their effects:

2. Please give the results of testing *(if any)*:

Please continue on a separate page if necessary

3. Please state if you consider that a transfer to C Wing, Parkhurst in particular would be appropriate and explain why:

4. Any other comments:

Name: Signature:

Position: Date:

Please continue on a separate page if necessary

82

Probation Officer's Report

1. Please give a brief account of the prisoner's current domestic circum-stances *(including any visits he may receive)*:

2. Any other comments *(comments on the prisoner's personal strengths and weaknesses and any specific problem areas would be of particular help)*:

Name: Signature:

Position: Date:

Please continue on a separate page if necessary

Specialist Report by _____ *(please specify)*

Name: Signature:

Position: Date:

Please continue on a separate page if necessary

Printed for Her Majesty's Stationery Office by Commercial Colour Press, London E7. 5/87, C20, Dd.240221.